D1260094

DUBCEK SPEAKS

DUBCEK SPEAKS

Alexander Dubcek
with Andras Sugar

I.B. Tauris & Co Ltd
Publishers
London · New York

Published in 1990 by
I.B. Tauris & Co Ltd
110 Gloucester Avenue
London NW1 8JA

175 Fifth Avenue
New York
NY 10010

Distributed in the United States of America and Canada by
St Martin's Press
175 Fifth Avenue
New York
NY 10010

British Library Cataloguing in Publication Data
Dubcek, Alexander
Dubcek speaks.
1. Czechoslovakia. Invasion by Warsaw Pact countries.
Political aspects.
I. Title. II. Sugar, Andras
943.7042

ISBN 1–85043–208–2

Printed and bound in Great Britain by
Redwood Press Limited, Melksham, Wiltshire

ACKNOWLEDGEMENTS

The publishers would like to thank John Rehor for his advice on the political and historical background to the events in the book, Kathy Szent-Gyorgyi for her help and translation work. Thanks also to Edith Adler and Elizabeth Ger.

PUBLISHERS'
PREFACE

Alexander Dubcek's lengthy interview with Andras Sugar, screened twice by Hungarian television on 17 and 26 April 1989, must be counted as part of the remarkable chain of events that led up to the 1989 revolutions in Eastern Europe. This book reproduces the full text of that discussion in English for the first time. It was conducted in Czech and broadcast with a Hungarian voice-over that did not obscure the original, and so was picked up and understood by the people of southern Slovakia who were able to tune in to Budapest television.

In both countries Dubcek's interview caused a sensation. Media comment in Czechoslovakia was hostile. *Rude Pravo*, the Communist Party daily, accused Dubcek of deceiving the Hungarian public much as he had deceived the Czechoslovak CP leadership in 1968. The Czechoslovak Ambassador to Hungary expressed surprise in his talks with the Hungarian Minister and high-ranking Party official, Rezsoe Nyers, that Dubcek had been allowed to appear on Hungarian TV presenting what he claimed were historically incorrect, groundless and subjective views. Czechoslovak television accused Hungarian television of bad taste akin to its recent showing of the renowned Italian MP and porno star, La Cicciolina, accompanying the departure of a section of Soviet troops from Hungary.

In Hungary Andras Sugar tried to publish the full text in book form, but the then Secretary of State for Culture stopped the publication. Sugar wrote a scathing attack on the decision in *Reform*, the Budapest weekly, with the result that the Secretary of State was forced to resign, book censorship was abolished in Hungary and *Dubcek Megszolal* was published.

After the Soviet invasion, Dubcek was effectively silenced and retreated to a quiet life as a forestry worker in Bratislava. His political position in 1968 is often forgotten and, in the years that followed the invasion, he was criticised by many for the part he had played, or failed to play, in the events of 1968. However, there was no doubt of his enormous popularity in 1968. In spite of the fact that he represented a discredited communist party, public opinion polls in that year showed that almost 90 per cent of Czechoslovak citizens backed Dubcek. They supported his programme of building democratic socialism, and only 5 per cent wanted a return to capitalism.

On 30 October 1989 Hungarian television transmitted another interview with Alexander Dubcek. Less than three weeks later Dubcek took part in the student demonstration in Prague held to mark the 50th anniversary of a similar student demonstration against the occupying Nazi forces. The peaceful event was brutally suppressed by the police and Dubcek himself was detained briefly. But within a week the Stalinist regime in Czechoslovakia was swept away. The next time Alexander Dubcek came to Prague was to appear on a balcony in Wenceslas Square on 24 November. Standing alongside Vaclav Havel, he announced: 'Praguers, I hope you're glad to see me back . . .' and was given an enthusiastic and emotional reception by an enormous crowd. This tall, frail figure turning 68 had been overtaken by the events of November 1989, but remained a symbol of popular democracy for Czechoslovakia.

INTRODUCTION

Snorting and wheezing, the television company's old Volga ascends the 21-degree slope of Lermontov Street, by the side of Bratislava Castle. A few turns. The crew from the 'Panorama' programme of the television foreign affairs department has arrived at the destination set two days earlier. It is 12 April 1989.

We are already standing in front of no.31, Misikivo Street, the home of Alexander Dubcek. I glance down at the city. My God, I was also here on 21 August 1968!

At that time I was the London correspondent of the Bratislava *Uj Szo*, 'on a private basis'. In other words, as the London correspondent of the Hungarian Telegraph Agency, every afternoon I briefly sent by telex the most interesting news, often my own comments, in reports to the Bratislava paper for the Magyar minority resident there. *Uj Szo* paid for this, though not very generously; my fees accumulated nicely over the year, and each summer I dashed over, by train, to the Slovak capital in order to reap the yield of my work for the year, as well as to discuss with the editors their requirements and comments.

On this occasion, a room had been booked for me in the

Carlton Hotel, very near the Danube, on Hviezdoslav Square. On the evening of 20 August I had supper with the members of the editorial staff in a Slovak restaurant, and of course we discussed how Brezhnev would react to the democratic developments in Czechoslovakia.

'I am very well informed, since I spoke with Dubcek yesterday,' said Gyula Lorincz, the well-known painter, member of the presidium of the Slovak Communist Party, and incidentally editor-in-chief of *Uj Szo*. 'They won't come in, since the entire Soviet general staff has gone on leave. In this heat-wave, the top brass are spending their summer holidays on the Crimea, in Georgia. Anyway: the Bratislava meeting on 3 August ended with very fine results, in a good atmosphere . . .' This was the meeting at which the 'five' (the leaders of the Soviet, Hungarian, Bulgarian, Polish and GDR Communist Parties) were last with Dubcek; they had walked on the streets, shaken hands with passers-by in Bratislava which was bathed in sunshine . . .

Since I wanted to get up early the following day, 21 August, in order to travel home by train, I went to bed in the Carlton quite soon after supper. Soon I sank into a deep sleep, but all at once, at around 1.30 a.m., I was wakened by the sound of a terribly loud helicopter. It was as if the infernal machine was roaring in my room!

'Damn them, can't they, in the dead of night, fly anywhere else other than over the Danube?' Muttering this, I got myself to sleep half an hour later.

The alarm-clock went off at 5 a.m. I packed my things. On the way downstairs, I became aware of a lanky man rushing past me with a transistor radio pressed to his ear. I heard these words from the radio '. . . Kl ud a rozvahu', which means calm and level-headedness in Slovak.

Then someone else came on the radio, this time in Hungarian, and I recognized the well-known voice of the

Radio Free Europe news-reader. Some sort of communiqué was being outlined on behalf of the Czechoslovak Communist Party and Government, but I did not hear the rest of it.

After breakfast, I stepped out on to Hviezdoslav Square. From the right, five or six sand-coloured tanks, painted with white stripes but with no national markings, rolled into the square and stopped. These Czechoslovak soldiers have gone mad, I thought. Bringing tanks into the city centre because of some summer exercise. Scarcely had I finished thinking this, when the top of the tank opened, and a Mongoloid-faced young soldier climbed out, carrying a machine-gun; shaking, he looked around.

That was when I cottoned on. It appears that it is not the Czechs who have gone crazy, I said to myself.

I left my suitcase in the hotel foyer, and set off for my Bratislava friends. They informed me about the developments, which since then the entire world knows: the troops of the five had entered Czechoslovakia; there was no armed resistance; Dubcek had disappeared; radio and television were transmitting live their entry and the protests . . .

I went to the Square of the Slovak National Uprising (SNP Square for short), which was once Stalin Square. There was an enormous crowd, and tanks here and there. Young people were shouting in unison: 'Dubcek, Svoboda! To je nasa sloboda!' Meaning: 'Dubcek, Svoboda, they are our freedom!'

They sang the national anthem, the first part of which was a dignified, slow Czech national song, and the second a lively Slovak tune. Then they chanted again.

I learned that the border was closed, that even Hungarian troops were coming.

It was afternoon, already. I looked into the Hungarian

consulate-general on Palisady Street. There was a small hole in the heavy iron gate which was closed. After I had rung for a long time, it was opened with great difficulty, and someone cautiously peeked out. I introduced myself. 'I should like to speak to comrade Consul Pal Sztanko,' I said. 'You can't, comrade Sztanko is sleeping', said the unknown person, and the gate was already closing.

Let us leave the consul to sleep ... A young Magyar lad from Somorja,* almost in tears, said: 'Are you mad, to have come here with tanks? You will leave in the end, anyway, but we shall remain here!'

There was nothing more I could do. I had to go back to the Carlton, and set myself up for a stay lasting a good number of days, since the border was closed. Fortunately, I had a few thousand Korunas.

In Hungarian, I told the girl at the reception desk that I could not go home, and that I would like my room back for a few days. She retorted angrily: 'You came in with tanks, I have nothing to discuss with you!' and withdrew. Five minutes later she returned. I looked deep into her eyes: 'Little girl, I came not by tank, but by train. Anyway, I live in London. And you can't know what my opinion is of the whole thing.' Her attitude softened, and without saying anything she pressed the key into my hand.

A young lady, a total stranger, was sitting upstairs in my room. Who knows whether it was in error, but she had been given my room. She introduced herself: Carola Kilstrom, correspondent of Swedish radio, from Stockholm. She offered me a chair, and we chatted in English. 'Well, tell me, Carola, what fine things have you been able to get hold of for Swedish radio?'

---

*A town in Slovakia, mainly inhabited by Magyars; called Samorin in Slovak.

Miss Kilstrom flushed with enthusiasm: 'Imagine, I was given a colossal interview by Eugen Suchon, the greatest Slovak composer!'

'And what did the composer talk about?'

'You won't believe this: about the relationship between Slovak folk songs and written music, about their inter-relationship! Sensational!!!'

'I congratulate you. And tell me, Carola, are you by any chance making any report on the invasion?'

Her Swedish eyes open wide:

'What invasion?'

'Well, haven't you seen the tanks?'

'Oh, those! Of course I've seen them. But there are always tanks on the street in a communist country . . .'

'Well, then pay attention . . .' – and I told her in detail what was happening in Czechoslovakia.

With sudden eagerness, Carola slung her reporter's tape-recorder over her shoulder and jumped up, saying: 'Come with me! Let's go to the tanks!'

We set off. I told Carola that I would follow three paces behind her, that I would help if there were any problems, but that she should not expect the London correspondent of MTI, who was on holiday, to provide her with 'substantive' assistance. If I did, in Budapest I would be kicked out of my job. Did dear Carola understand that?

Miss Kilstrom stepped over to one of the tanks, on top of which a young Soviet lieutenant was explaining to the protesting Slovak people, young and old: 'Mi prijehali na manyovri . . . We have come for manoeuvres, do you understand?' (Carola was recording everything.)

Strident laughter. The lieutenant continued, and Carola stuck the microphone virtually into his mouth. The young officer became angry, and shouted at her: 'Uberi mikrafon! . . . take away that microphone!'

Carola was visibly frightened, but then she pulled herself together and addressed the crowd, in German: 'Gentlemen, those who know both German and Russian, please translate for this sympathetic officer that Sweden is a neutral country, a friend of the Soviet Union. Premier Kosygin was Sweden's guest a few weeks ago and signed a very fine communiqué . . . I am a Swedish journalist and I am doing my job.'

The young Slovaks translated animatedly. The officer drew himself up and turned into a diplomat. He patiently explained to Carola: 'Da, mi znajem . . . Yes, we know that Sweden is a neutral and friendly country. We also know that comrade Kosygin was there. But what are you doing here, since you are a foreigner!'

There was even more strident laughter. 'And what are you: Czech, or perhaps Slovak?' several people shouted to the lieutenant.

Carola put down her microphone; she gestured happily that we should go back to the Carlton to listen to the interview.

It then emerged that when the officer had shouted at her, Carola had instinctively turned off the microphone. The whole beautiful conversation about the Swedish, and about Kosygin . . . had slipped away into oblivion.

'You're an unlucky girl', I said. 'I imagine that when you return home the managing-director of Swedish radio will be there waiting at Stockholm airport, and he will ask where is the big report on the invasion, and you will happily reply that there is none, but that there is a sensational interview with Eugen Suchon about folk music. And you will whizz out of Swedish radio, straight into the famous, protective net of Swedish welfare . . .'

Carola became more eager: 'Let's go back to the tanks! I'll record it again, and many additional minutes' worth as well!' 'Just go, but on your own. And God bless.'

After that, I went through the streets on my own. The

special edition of *Uj Szo* had already been published; it, too, protested against the invasion. In the editorial office they said that if the protest had not been published, the windows would most probably have been smashed. Of course, my colleagues agreed with the protest, they were not at all happy and were fearful about the future.

An enormous crowd was surging on SNP Square, even at ten o'clock in the evening, arguing with the armed soldiers. The Russian soldiers were obviously very tired, since everyone was offering them cigarettes, but nothing else. They would have liked a glass of water, but there was none.

I addressed a Russian major who was passing by: 'I have heard that you have called a curfew from eight o'clock in the evening. Then why are there so many people on the streets?' 'Because you are so undisciplined!' he shouted, and went on.

From one of the tanks, a soldier was explaining: 'Understand this: I have taken in everything, indeed, I agree with you! But I cannot hand over my arms, or the tank. Understand this! You are right! Just give me a glass of water!'

'Not that, but you can have cigarettes.'

. . . With great difficulty, I got home the next day.

A few years later, I was making a film-report in Moscow. On the left hand of the Russian colleague who was briefing me, I noticed a tattoo, in Roman letters, between the thumb and forefinger: PRAHA 1968.

To my question, he replied ashamedly: 'Well, yes, I was there, and it was the madness of youth: I let them tattoo me. But I am very fed up with it. Everyone asks: "Aren't you ashamed, that you were there, and yet you even show it off?"'

'How can that be? Isn't it considered to be an honour?' I asked ingenuously.

'Honour?' He waved his hand. 'Hell, no. It was a big failure, shame and disgrace. That's what everyone here thinks.'

And now, at three o'clock in the afternoon of 12 April 1989, here I am, standing in front of Alexander Dubcek's villa. Standing beside me, with camera, lamps, supporting stand, are Jozsef Marton, cameraman, Zsolt Hegyi, who is in charge of filming, and fellow-journalist Laszlo Liszkai. We ring the bell.

A lady with blond dyed hair looks out of the upstairs window. I recognize her from earlier photographs: Anna Dubcekova, Alexander's wife, and mother of three sons. She looks surprisingly youthful.

She calls out: 'Who are you and what do you want?' As soon as I say: Hungarian Television, she replies joyfully: 'Wait, I'll come down.' We tell her what we have come for. Madame Anna goes up, soon the buzzer sounds, and we open the gate.

Dubcek comes out to meet us, he helps to take in the enormous amount of paraphernalia. His little white dog greets us in a friendly manner. Dubcek himself is visibly pleased at the visitors. He says a few words in Hungarian, with a surprisingly good accent. Nevertheless, we speak in Russian, rather; as we shall see from the interview, he learned this language in Kirgiziya and Gorky.

The several-storey villa looks as if it were in any prosperous suburb; here it is on the slope of Castle hill in Bratislava and the name of the street is Misikova. The birds are singing, the fruit trees are in blossom; it's an idyllic setting. The interior of the house is quite crowded, there are many knick-knacks, and even more books; it is like the flat of an intellectual from Buda, in the golden age of the 1940s. Even the aroma of the dwelling is that 'good smell of a flat in Buda'.

We set up the camera, the lamps. Meanwhile Dubcek explains: he does not allow secret police into the house, but sometimes it is obvious that they are watching him. Otherwise, he goes about the city freely; he can travel to Prague, anywhere. He was still working not long ago, at the forestry enterprise, but he is now retired.

DUBCEK SPEAKS

[We switch on the two 1,000 watt lamps. Cameraman Jozsef Marton turns on the Betacam motion picture camera. I ask the first question in my mother-tongue.]

Can we speak in Hungarian?
[Dubcek smiles:] In Hungarian? I used to know a bit, but I was never very good at speaking the language. I worked in Banska Bystrica, where I was a principal secretary. [This is how he speaks, with this precision, and with a surprisingly good Hungarian accent.] I had a chauffeur, Tibor, with whom I could speak in Hungarian, and when I went in to work, I said: 'Tibor, dobre rano', and Tibor replied: 'Not dobre rano, I wish you good morning.' I said: 'Well then, good morning'.

Then let us continue in Slovak. You will reply in Slovak, while I ask the questions in Russian, all right?
[He nods.]

How did your personality develop, from the very beginning?
My life was quite difficult. Quite a lot of serious problems have left their mark on my age-group, the current sixty-year-olds. We have lived through many things, or one could say that we

have lived at a relatively quick pace – the reason being that, since the First World War, mankind has gone through many kinds of changes and has taken part in many upheavals and much tribulation. All this has not happened without leaving a trace. At the time of the Second World War, during the period of the victory of socialism and the period of the distortions of socialism ... well, this was a very complex time. My life developed in accordance with the way these events took place.

I was born into a working-class family; my father was a cabinet-maker, his younger sister was a seamstress and both of them learned their trades in Budapest. During his apprenticeship, my father encountered the first revolutionary stirrings, because, after all, in the years prior to the First World War Budapest was considered to be the revolutionary centre for Slovakia and the other neighbouring regions. My father grew up during the time that social democracy began to function. Since you have asked how my life developed, I cannot leave out this information.

Before the First World War, my father went to America, as a young man, after he had learned his trade. I believe he was in America from 1910–12 – unfortunately I don't know exactly, I have not had the chance to look into it – up to 1921. It was there that he became acquainted with my mother, who had gone out there to her elder sisters; they had paid her passage on the ship, or – as they called it then – the 'siffkarta'. My mother at that time was about 15 years old. Thus, she got to know my father, and my father's life took shape in America; later on he also worked there in the trade union movement and lived a normal sort of American life. Of course, our people are good honest workers. He earned a good wage as an artisan during this period, and planned to return eventually to Czechoslovakia to set himself up independently. So he came back in the Spring of 1921, with the entire family.

My older brother was born in Chicago; he was only eighteen months older than me.

You were almost born in America, too, isn't that so?
Well, my parents returned home in the Spring, and since I was born on 27 November and my parents came back sometime in March, my beginning, my conception, really took place out there. You won't believe this, but I have only once mentioned this, in reply to a journalist's question, and now, quite recently, a few weeks ago, a long article was published in *Rude Pravo* and *Bratislava Pravda*, in which once again, as continually over the past 20 years, efforts were made to discredit me, both as a person and as a politician, in the eyes of our people and world public opinion, and they used the information which I believe I had given to a correspondent of the American magazine *Life* – or Voice of America? – that my roots were to be sought in America. It's hard to believe that *Rude Pravo* would publish such a thing – however sarcastically. Of course, I was unable to influence my parents! I only gave this information once, somewhere, as a statistic from my life. I have my own opinion of these ideologists who claim that they are Marxists, Leninists, and who knows what. In my opinion, they are rather base people, they are not civilized . . . and they abuse this statistic! They have it published in *Rude Pravo*! As if I had boasted of it! I had only stated a fact. When I think of it . . . they are 'propagandists' – of course in quotation marks – and were they working somewhere in the United States, they might investigate how the roots of my opportunism and revisionism or, Heaven forbid, my relationship to imperialism, stem from America, because that is where I was conceived. They are capable of many things. They made a sarcastic, ironic comment even out of this. In my view our people condemn this sort of thing, but our propaganda grabs at everything possible. In the next such article, perhaps they will say the following:

'So here you are, his roots, the roots of his opportunism, his revisionism go back to the United States of America.'

Serious people don't take this seriously . . . And then your father went to work in the Soviet Union, didn't he?
Well, initially he wanted to work here at home, since he had money and would have liked to open an independent workshop. But abroad he had already taken part in the workers' movement, and when he came back, the wave of the workers' movement was growing around these parts, in connection with the formation of the communist parties. My father became one of the founder members of the Czechoslovak Communist Party, and was the first chairman of the party organization in Uhrovce (Ugroc), where I was born.

Which district is that in?
Uhrovce is in the Topolcany district, in Slovakia. My father was therefore a participant in this revolutionary movement. In Soviet Russia, great things were happening, and after the Communist Party was formed, an appeal was published asking for specialists to go to the Soviet Union to assist the industrialization there.

Was this the Interhelpo?*
Yes, Interhelpo. My father also applied, and as a self-aware socialist, a communist, he bought machinery and equipment out of his earnings, he invested everything in this – and he took it to the Soviet Union, to this co-operative, practically as a gift. That was our family's contribution to the industrialization in 1925.

*Interhelpo: 1925–43, a co-operative founded by Czech and Slovak workers and farmers, near the city of Frunze in Soviet Kirghizia, as an expression of international help to the young Soviet state.

And in which town did you end up?
In Frunze; at that time this central Asian town was still called
Pispek. People from various nations lived there: Czechs,
Slovaks, Hungarians, Germans, etc. Of course, they were all
communists.

How long were you there?
Till 1938.

And were you caught up in the Yezhovite* terror of 1937?
In the Soviet Union, I lived through all of these ominous years,
but also through many pleasurable moments too. There were
some of the latter. For example, a textile factory was built by
our co-operative, a leather-processing factory was built, and
a large furniture-manufacturing works was also created. The
co-operative was a large organization, in which we ourselves
made everything, from bread to machines, to machine-repairs.
A large cultural centre was built there, and schools too. We built
our own houses. Initially we had settled on a large plain, and
our parents built all these things. I remember that when I was
little boy, we were late in starting to attend school, because
we could do so only after we had built the school. All of us,
ten-year-olds, six-year-olds, eight-year-olds, were in the same
class. To this very day the town is proud of its cultural centre,
because it really is of as very high standard, – the work of a
master, since it was built by masters like my father who had
learnt his trade in Budapest, and many others. You can well
imagine the standard to which the centre was built at that time,
in Central Asia . . . In the town of Frunze, and elsewhere, too,

---

*Nikolay Yezhov, Soviet security chief from 1936–8, carried out the most severe stage
of the great Stalinist purges, cruelly and ruthlessly eliminating Stalin's enemies ranging
from prominent Party leaders to the general population.

there were other premises, factories, and so on. Everything was done to a very high professional standard, and people from our country enjoyed great esteem there.

What influenced your family to return home to Czecho-slovakia? Moreover, before the war?

The year 1938 came, and as you know, my father had functioned in the Communist (Bolshevik) Party of the Soviet Union, where he had been an official. The period set in when the Fascists came to power. Earlier, there had been great repression in the USSR; you are already well aware of this, and on the basis of the current press as well. Others who were capable of working politically left the Soviet Union to carry on political activity elsewhere. My father was amongst them. In 1938, he came back to Czechoslovakia bringing me with him, and here he participated in underground activity as a member of the leadership of the illegal Communist Party. He worked in this way till 1944; in 1944 he was arrested and taken to Mauthausen.

Was this the time of the so-called Slovak State?*

Partly. The first Czechoslovak Republic [set up in 1918] was still in existence in 1938–9, but Fascism was emerging, and preparations for later events were under way; we lived through the year 1938 as the end of the Republic, as the beginning of its disintegration. Earlier you enquired about the repression in the Soviet Union. Of course, I lived through that period as a young man there. I remember, as if it were yesterday what

---

*The Slovak State, or more correctly the Slovak Republic, was proclaimed on 14 March 1939 after the disintegration of the Czechoslovak Republic. It was a fascist state allied to Nazi Germany, and finally collapsed following Germany's defeat in 1945.

textbooks were like at the time the Tukhachevsky* trial took place [in 1937]. If I am not wrong, on the left-hand page of the textbook he could be seen in ceremonial finery, and we learned about him as a great military leader. Later on, however, we were taught that he was a traitor, and at that time we had to cut out that page . . .

Because he had become an 'enemy of the people'?
The page had to be handed in, at the time of the trials. Later on other similar procedures took place, which affected many economists and, as I remember, many political elements: Bukharin and all the others, Rykov etc. I remember those trials very well, they took place in the 1930s, when I was growing up, and naturally the effect of the trials was that one somehow did not understand the whole thing. I would in no way be telling the truth if I were to say that 'I already knew at the time' . . .

No. But since I lived through similar events in the 1950s in this country, Czechoslovakia, and later myself experienced, and still do experience, similar things, – and I witnessed Khrushchev's coming to power in 1956, since at that time I was studying in the Party academy in the Soviet Union – it is not surprising that these things combined to influence how one's political attitude, political actions and political stances took shape, and profoundly influenced one's moral aspect. I developed and grew up amidst all this; Initially it had a great impact, a great influence, on me, and when I was able to influence our country's political life, it was not surprising that I adhered so stubbornly to my views, not just in 1968 but in the time that has elapsed since then. Because I understood

*Commander-in-Chief of the Red Army, Marshal Tukhachevsky was the Soviet Union's most outstanding military leader. He fell victim to Stalin during the great purge of army officers in 1937.

that socialism had to be reformed, that it had to acquire a new content, a new form and that it had to become much more attractive than ever before. Otherwise it had no future.

It is said that you came to this conclusion when you fought as a Slovak patriot against Czech predominance in the Novotny period [1957–68]* . . . Or were these perhaps two entirely separate processes in your psychological development?

I would say that all these things had a joint effect gradually, one after the other. My process of growing up was concluded when I graduated from the Moscow Party college and returned home in 1959, as well as when I worked as county Party Secretary in Bratislava. By 1960 I was already a Secretary of the Central Committee of the Czechoslovak Communist Party (CPCZ) in Prague, with responsibility for industry. I am a mechanic by profession, so I took part in the direction of the engineering industry and in the chemical and construction industries. And naturally, in those days, after graduating from the political college and after Khrushchev's rise to power, these events had an effect on me. And certain things, which I experienced as a District Party Secretary were hard to tolerate. Of course, at that time I did not know all that I learnt, when I was Central Committee Secretary, about Slansky† and about the trials that were carried out in our country in the early 1950s.

*The posts of the Party leader and President were combined from 1948 when Gottwald was elected the first Communist President of Czechoslovakia. The same applied to his successors, Zapotocky and Novotny. One of the first moves of the reform movement of 1968 was to separate these two posts with Dubcek becoming the First Secretary and Novotny remaining President until subsequently forced to resign. This was reversed in the Seventies when these two posts were once again combined under Husak.

†Rudolf Slansky was the Party's General Secretary from 1945 to 1951 while Gottwald held the more important post of Party Chairman. In 1951 Slansky was stripped of his post and made Vice-Premier, a largely nominal post. In that year he was arrested, tried on trumped up charges of treason, and executed a year later. He was rehabilitated in 1963.

When I worked as District Party Secretary in 1949 and 1950, during the time of the first arrests, naturally as a young communist, an enthusiastic follower of socialism, I could not understand how it was possible that after so many years certain communists were found to be enemies of the people. However, the propaganda was working at full strength. And certain facts were made use of. Certain evidence had come to light, it was said, which suggested that they were traitors, that they had co-operated with the imperialists, with imperialist agents. Of course, as District Party Secretary one asked oneself the question: how was it possible for them to operate for so long in the Party, without anyone unmasking them? Naturally, it is not possible to appear as if one might at that time already have been so wise as to understand everything. If I thought back to what I had experienced in the Soviet Union, of course I felt that many things did not add up. But such 'traitors' were also unmasked in the Hungarian Communist Party, for example, and in the other communist parties. The propaganda worked in the way that was intended: the hand of imperialism had penetrated deeply into the communist movement. Moreover, the following version was drummed into our heads: bourgeois propaganda and imperialism work in the long term, on the basis of a long-term plan. This is why people were planted amongst the communists at the time of the birth of the communist movement. Therefore, we went so far as to accept even such blatant lies. This is a tragedy. It's difficult to talk about it, but I am sure that, by about 1963, after Novotny had sent me back to Slovakia, I was already considered to be rather a difficult man. There were small, rather than large, conflicts on many practical matters, on matters related to implementing policy in Prague.

I came back to Slovakia from the position of CPCZ Central Committee Secretary – which was, of course, a higher position than Secretary of the Slovak Communist Party's

Central Committee – on the grounds that it was necessary to strengthen the party here, that young people were needed. I became one of the Secretaries of the Central Committee of the Slovak Communist Party.

Was Viliam Siroky* still in Bratislava at that time?
Viliam Siroky was not in power any more. He was premier up to the end of the 1950s. Then he was replaced by Lenart, who became premier during Novotny's time. Siroky was not active any more. But in the 1950s he was chairman of the Slovak Communist Party. And at that time I was already working in the Party apparatus, indeed in the Central Committee apparatus.

And how was your becoming First Secretary received here in the Bratislava apparatus?
Well, some time passed before I took on the position of First Secretary. I came back to Slovakia in 1962, and then became First Secretary in 1963. If you had observed the action I took then, what my conduct was like, what I did, you would have seen that I tried to pursue a policy which would be to the benefit of the Communist Party, not just to the Party, but also to the people as a whole. The result of this was, inter alia, that in a relatively short time I gained quite a lot of popularity. I say this sincerely, although it may perhaps sound strange coming from my mouth, but I did not do this in order to pursue some kind of popular policy. I am this type of person. When I worked in a factory, or in the district, or in the county, I don't know why, but I very much liked working with people, I was

---

*Viliam Siroky was a prominent Slovak Communist: he was Czechoslovak Prime Minister from 1953 until 1963 when he was forced to resign Party and government posts because of shortcomings in his work and political mistakes he had made.

able to form good relations with them, and vice versa. Wherever I have worked, I don't know why, but I have obtained considerable respect; people have acknowledged me. Perhaps the reason is that wherever I worked, whoever I talked to, I never made them feel that I was more important than the person I was talking to, or who turned to me for help.

So you have never acted superciliously?
No, I have never done that. And this is possibly one of the reasons for my popularity. In his memoirs, Vasil Bilak* – two or three such works of his have been published – says that, in Slovakia, I was working towards becoming First Secretary. Seeing I was a Central Committee Secretary, it was logical that I should not act so that Novotny would perhaps send me packing. Had I done so, I would have been completely naive! Of course, I soon became First Secretary. Bilak writes that, all right, Novotny put me forward for this position! Well, if he was First Secretary of the CPCZ, this was his job, stemming from his position. But when I was elected First Secretary of the Slovak Communist Party, Novotny did not even wait for the end of the session. I asked him to wait until the end of the session. But he did not stay, because . . . well, because if you are compelled to act, but not as your heart tells you, you at least make this known by leaving the assembly-hall.

*Vasil Bilak was a hardline Slovak Communist who, in 1968, succeeded Dubcek as First Secretary of the Slovak Communist Party. He maintained behind Dubcek's back secret contacts with the Soviet Party leadership. In August 1968 he was stripped of his Party posts but reinstated soon afterwards after Soviet pressure. He then remained a leading member of the Party membership and pursued hardline policies until his retirement in 1989.

31

In January 1968 you were elected First Secretary of the Central Committee of the entire Czechoslovak Communist Party. How did this decision affect you, when all of a sudden you gained such a high post, not only in Slovakia but at the front line of the whole of Czechoslovakia?

Well, you know, this is an important moment in a person's life. I felt a very great sense of responsibility. The way in which I was elected has been very much simplified these days. Indeed, Bilak even writes: 'What! Is this person now talking about some kind of renewal, when in 1968 Novotny put him forward to the Central Committee as candidate for First Secretary?!' This is only a half-truth. And half-truths always border on lies and demagoguery . . .

They say that it's even worse . . .

Yes, you're right, it is worse than lying. Because look: I got into sharp confrontation with Novotny at the 1967 October plenum where we were evaluating the work of the Party. At that time most of the speakers had prepared their customary contributions. I said to myself, since I have been in Slovakia, I have already built a few of the new elements into the policy based on the leading role of the Party and I have discovered a lot of new things in the nationality policy. I was thinking of my relations with the Hungarian and Ukrainian nationalities living in Slovakia. I had made observations regarding certain elements of the so-called 'Slovak issue'* and naturally I tried to put them into practice in the work of the higher authorities as well. As regards my election in 1968, it was not a matter of my nomination having been so easy, of Novotny having accepted me so easily.

---

*The 'Slovak issue' refers to resentment felt in Slovakia about too great a concentration of power in Prague, and the arrogant and high-handed attitude to Slovaks by the then Party leader and President, Novotny.

In 1967 I attacked the previous policy because I was dissatisfied with it. That is when I formulated the most important and most determinant point, that the Party must work according to a programme – since it had no programme up to then. For this reason, it had to elaborate a new political programme; the Party could not govern, the Party had to lead. The Government's task is to govern. And if one wants to lead, that can be done only on the basis of some kind of programme. And the people who are to be led should voluntarily follow the Party. In other words, leading and governing are not the same thing. If we say that the Party must lead, this means that it must exercise its leading role on the basis of a deep knowledge of the party programme, indeed, I might say on the basis of a scientifically developed party programme. This is why scholars dealing with all the various spheres of life must take part in shaping the party programme. Sociologists, economists, political scientists must be involved . . . in other words, the party's policy must be placed on scientific foundations. For this reason, I took the line in 1968 that the Party must work out a new political programme, that we were living in a different period, the scientific-technical revolution was under way in the world, the Party could not govern as it had been doing.

And in 1967 I argued that if we criticize the government for not governing, this also means self-criticism at the same time, self-criticism by the CPCZ Central Committee. Because if the governing is not done by the government, but by the Party apparatus, in other words, the Central Committee, then self-criticism has to be exercised urgently and this policy has to be changed. You can perhaps imagine the reaction to this.

There is not enough time here and now to reproduce my entire speech verbatim, but among the stereotyped texts which the Central Committee was accustomed to, it exploded like a bombshell. Of course, I was not allowed to finish my speech; Novotny interrupted me; the microphones were switched off;

he called his secretary over and made her sit in the front row. Novotny's chief propagandist, Hendrych, immediately delivered a speech against me, saying that I wanted to weaken the leading role of the Party. Finally Novotny also spoke and accused me of nationalism. In fact, I had not brought up any nationality questions; I only spoke about the problems that could be experienced in Slovakia.

Well, it was in this atmosphere that my election was prepared. And if you were to ask me how this happened, I would answer that of course, I knew that the situation in Bohemia and Slovakia and throughout the country, was complicated. It was not that I might perhaps not have understood it. I had worked as a Central Committee Secretary, I had lived through the abolition of the first republic, the re-birth of the republic, the first years of building the new country. I had completed college, I was familiar with the life and work of the people – of course, I saw the problems: what the people, the Party, the whole society needed. But I thought that the best thing would be for a Czech to be appointed First Secretary. And those who are currently in leading positions in the country are well aware that during the entire period of the three Central Committee sessions, that is, from October to December and from December to January, when in the end the choice fell on me, I was all the time working in the corridors, amongst county delegates, in the Presidium [in current parlance, the Politburo], everywhere where it was possible to exert any influence, so that Oldrich Cernik, who was Czech, should be elected First Secretary. He was already a Central Committee Secretary. Before that he had been a county council chairman, and had also functioned as a minister, as chairman of the Planning Office. So he was prepared for this position, and I did my utmost to get him elected. But you know how it is . . . it was a difficult birth. The December session of the Central Committee was even stormier, all the more so because I was accused of nationalism. Stirrings also began in Slovakia. This did not please the Czech communists, they saw that things were developing in an unexpected direction. And the debate assumed an entirely different character, because everything revolved around the dissatisfaction with the Party's work. Even the work of the Presidium was criticized!

In the end a committee was set up, to which the county delegations elected representatives. In connection, I observed that this was the first move towards the democratic election of the First Secretary. This committee called for nominations. There were five or six: Dubcek, Lenart, Cernik, Lastovicka, and even more were mentioned. The plenary session of the Central Committee lasted until January, in three stages. Now they say that Novotny proposed me. But what else could he have done? He, too, had information from the plenum, from the conversations in the corridors, from the co-ordinating committee – this is what they called the committee which the plenum had elected democratically – because the plenum saw that there had been a loss of trust in the Presidium. The co-ordinating committee discussed all the candidates, and Novotny knew that it would propose me, Dubcek, at the plenum. Under the weight of this pressure, he was not so stupid or so naive as not to know that he had to support the candidate who was now being offered and whom the plenum would accept unanimously. So he acted as if it had been his own proposal. He quickly convened the Presidium, and the Presidium put me forward as a candidate. In other words, what happened was that, after the nomination by the committee, Novotny in the Presidium presented the result of the decision as his own, since he could do nothing else.

That is clear.

And at the plenum, he made the formal presentation. So Bilak makes use of this event against me, in a very demagoguical manner. Indeed, what is more, after my election, – since we are only human, – I objected to many things in Novotny's policy. However, my nature is such that I thought: he has now ended his career as First Secretary. When I stood up and prepared to leave the platform, naturally I had to go past him. He, too, stood up, turned towards me and held out his hand. He stretched out his hand and somehow drew me to him. Of course, the assembly also accepted this with understanding. Yet Bilak now makes use of this and writes: 'What do you want with Dubcek, since he, too, was pro-Novotny. Look at that hand-shake . . .' But what was important was what I did when I was able to work independently, and not what I was not able to do during my time as district or county Secretary.

[At this point the interviewer needs to make a sincere confession. One of the basic rules of our profession is that the subject of a report may be sympathetic or perfectly hateful, but we do not *express* antipathy or sympathy directly (but rather through 'metacommunication'). In this case, however, I had already come to like Dubcek so much during the first half hour, that I was forced to regard his polemical comments as entirely unnecessary. Why was this man apologizing and why was he defending himself against some stupid slander? And I admit that, without realizing it, I said what I was feeling.]

Don't take so much to heart what they say about this now, since the entire world knows that with your election an entirely new era began: you brought an end to what Novotny represented. You launched the Prague Spring.

I should like to turn now to the international aspect of events. Brezhnev reputedly said at the time: Our Sasha has come to power in Czechoslovakia, everything will be all right. Shortly afterwards, however, a certain tension began to characterize your relationship with Brezhnev and the Soviet leadership. Moscow made critical remarks about your policy. How did you sense the first indications that the Brezhnev leadership was not pleased with what you were doing, and did not want to understand it?

Look, here at home many people, even those who took part in the movement of renewal, try to make me appear as a person who was always influenced by someone, who was forced to do something, who did not have his own ideas for a programme . . .

And who was made use of . . .

That is the kind of image of me they try to create. Of course, these ideas were not formulated in a completely specific manner, but no one can take away from me the pioneering work which I did from the October 1967 plenum and onwards, or my speech delivered at the Central Committee plenum in February 1968, when I outlined the important elements towards elaborating the Action Programme. And no one can deny, practically until the Action Programme was elaborated, that I endeavoured primarily to work out a new political programme.

However, you have asked about Brezhnev. I have to tell you that neither then, nor in the period since, have I ever been anti-Soviet. On the contrary. If somebody from the age of four up to his adulthood is brought up in the environment that I was brought up in, and grows up among the companions that I had, well, it leaves an indelible mark on him for the whole of his life. And this naturally affected me too. I could not be anti-Soviet, I could not be the sort of anti-Soviet politician they have turned me into today. I feel whole-heartedly for the Soviet people. Why? Because I too have experienced the joy aroused by the completion of a hydroelectric power station, I have lived through the happiness of the workers of a car factory, because my father went from Frunze to work at the Gorky car factory. I went to school in that town and I have seen how many things grew and were built in that time and I also was happy about it. But, I was also aware of the poverty, the hunger, the collectivization. I have seen people dying of hunger, I have seen a lot.

So, I sympathize with the Soviet people; I could even be called a friend of the Soviet people, but if I say pro-Soviet, I mean that I was impressed by the policy started by Khrushchev. No matter what criticisms were levelled against him later, I respected him. In any case, he undertook pioneering work, and this made a great impact on me, as well as on the policy I chose. In the case of Brezhnev, naturally he was acquainted with me. They could not have known me as anything other than a person who could never be anti-Soviet; such a suggestion could only arise in the case of someone who was unknown. But I came out with a new political programme. And what contents that programme had! Early on, I mentioned only a few issues in connection with the Party, but issues concerning the relationship between the Party and the government, and the relationship of the Party to the people . . .

The human face . . .

. . . and I tried to formulate other things, too, and naturally to incorporate them in the programme. Enormous pressures weighed on me, both from the right and from the left. They thought someone had arrived on the scene who, in harmony with the image formed of me, was weak and naive. Possibly those on the Right thought: now we shall meet and distribute the lucrative jobs amongst ourselves. Possibly the sectarian-dogmatists believed: he will convene the Central Committee and we can finally settle our scores with the others. But I decided: there will be no such thing, neither the one, nor the other, nor a third! There will be a programme – and the programme will shape communist unity!

I could not have convened the Central Committee earlier. Many people say that I was late in convening it. Well, of course. But if I had convened it earlier there would only have been a big battle for power, for the spoils. And if there had not been a row over the spoils, if instead, let us say, there had been a political struggle between the progressive and the dogmatic sectarian wings, the people would not have understood this, and they would only have asked: now, what do they intend to do?

Therefore, as a politician, I had to learn that first and foremost, a programme was needed. And if the political battle continued, it would have to take place around some kind of programme. Therefore, this was the intention on which I acted: that it was necessary to work out a political programme. When we stated that the Party must be propped up in its work by scientific bases, this was put into practice. A group of 100–130 members of our scientific elite was formed and these scholars worked on the Party's programme. It was not surprising therefore that this programme was not only accepted by the Party, but that it genuinely became a programme of the people.

Was this the Action Programme?
Yes. The Action Programme was completed by April. The Soviets knew what was happening; they had information. I took vigorous action in February, and Brezhnev already sensed that I was preparing a programme whose contents contradicted the accepted rules of the time.

How did the first rumbles of thunder from the still-distant storm reach you? How did you notice the first signs that all this did not please Brezhnev and his associates?

Well, the first symptom, which was not entirely clear, was as follows. The February session of the Central Committee was held.

Nowadays I am criticized for supposedly letting Brezhnev dictate to me, for letting myself be influenced, and this was why I modified the text of my report. But that is not so. I took out two, three or four paragraphs – entire paragraphs, but in such a manner that the basic thought should not disappear. However, what were their objections? Look, I'm no longer able even to list them – matters concerning the situation of the Party, the working class, matters which are natural nowadays in Hungary, natural with Gorbachev. Of course, I left the basic thought in, and I thought: oops, this will be a big obstacle! But we had already set up the committees and we were working on the Action Programme. What gave rise therefore to my differences with Brezhnev was that he had information; I state this openly and unashamedly, that unfortunately that was the way the situation was then. They had their own people, I repeat, their own people, but I did not regard myself as being alien to them. But in this case 'own people' meant toadies – people who just kept their own advantage in mind and were not interested in the Party, the nation, the interests of society.

Intriguers, schemers . . .

So, after a time Brezhnev took note of us. I know now – but I did not know then – that he was secretly informed in some way that various things were being prepared in our country. Well, of course. And when the first, the Dresden meeting took place [in March 1968], I felt that, from the viewpoint of the Soviet leadership, the main problem lay with things related to our programme. Because, when the Moscow leadership of the

CPSU convened the Dresden meeting, I asked what was going to happen there. They said: we are only going to consult about economic matters, about this and that. Well, I said, all right, I shall talk then to the Prime Minister and the Chairman of the Planning Office. At that time, Lenart was Prime Minister and Cernik Chairman of the Planning Office.

So we went to Dresden. And everyone was there: Kadar, Gomulka, Ulbricht, Zhivkov* . . . the entire team, that is our team at the time. I sat down and I saw that I was facing a tribunal that was all ready for me. I thought: where have I ended up? I suddenly felt like Jan Hus at the Council of Constance. Well, was I before a tribunal or was I at a consultation of communist party leaders? And what else could I have done? At first I paid attention to what was being discussed, and then came all the questions: 'What is happening in your country? You have let go of the reins too much, you are not controlling things!'

Press freedom . . .

I said: 'we've abolished censorship.' To this they replied: 'Why are these things being written? And look what *is* being written!' And that this or that was anti-Soviet. But no, it was not anti-Soviet! And why such and such people held responsible positions, and what, how and why? And who was Jiri Pelikan?† I told them that Pelikan was the former chairman of the International Association of Students . . . And Pelikan

---

* Kadar, Gomulka, Ulbricht and Zhivkov were the respective Communist Party leaders of Hungary, Poland, East Germany and Bulgaria. Ulbrich and Gomulka were the most vociferous in pressing the Soviet leadership to take action against Dubcek's reformist regime, while Kadar played more of a moderating role.

† Jiri Pelikan as the Director General of Czechoslovak Television in 1968 was held jointly responsible for what Moscow called 'media excesses' during that period. Indeed, he was forced to resign in September 1968 following Soviet military intervention and pressure. He subsequently went into exile and became the publisher of the exile journal 'Listy' in Rome where he lives. He is now an Italian Socialist Party Euro-MP.

co-operated with various kinds of Soviet and other socialist youth and student movement leaders. He worked for years in this movement. He was a member of the CPCZ Central Committee. But why should I list all these things? . . .

Pelikan was the chairman of radio at that time, in 1968, wasn't he?
Yes. Then he became director of television. So this is how these things happened. It was very difficult.

And you couldn't do anything?
Look, this was in no way a consultation. It was an awkward meeting, which didn't even reach the level of a residents' association meeting. All very well if important things had been discussed; but to talk about what was happening here and what could and what could not be let out of our hands – these were not important things. But do you know what was important? That this questioning was merely the beginning; it was not the essence of the matter because they did not object to anything in our programme. But they had information about what the people preparing the Action Programme were working on. And this was what they were least able to explain. Propaganda is unable to cope with this to this very day. We adopted the Action Programme, but no evidence can be found that they might have taken action at any time against it. Why not? Because it would have meant that they were turning against the party programme. Instead, they charged: anti-Soviet forces, or forces of this or that type are gaining the opportunity to speak in your country. . . However, now, 20 years later, we know that the essence of the matter was not that someone spoke somewhere in a club, and said something which even I did not like at the time. We can't be so naive as to think that everyone believes in socialism. So there were some people who spoke out against it, and at Dresden they harped primarily on this aspect of events.

[The interview was being carried on in a strange way. A Betacam cassette lasts slightly longer than 20 minutes. Sometimes, we 'ran out' at the most interesting part. At these times, Dubcek – who said what he had to say in a rather passionate, sometimes vehement way, (and I admit, every interviewer dreams of such a subject) – noted his last sentence and carried on after the cassette change, where he had left off.

We were now in the thick of things, more and more important testimony was given about the details of the last great international frontal attack of Stalinism, about the steam-roller-like, unshakeable, rumbling pace of Brezhnev, who was still in good health, towards August 1968. . . . The interviewer tried to ask concrete, and if possible personal, questions. Here and there it was not easy to get a word in, for Dubcek carried on his epic surging performance with passion and profound conviction.

He was like an accused man, who had been unfairly sentenced 20 years earlier, and before whom an opportunity had now at last opened up to expound the truth.]

In Dresden, did you not notice any difference between Brezhnev and Kosygin, or say Kadar and Ulbricht? Was there no difference between them?
In order to know their personalities, their individual merits, what, for example, they did not reveal, I would have had to know them better, and not just on the basis of one or two conversations. And, I would have had to know not only what they said, but also what they did. In other words, I didn't know their individual natures very well at all. However, I would like to say the following: I think there was a big difference between them, as regards their tactical attitude, their outward reaction to what was said. Naturally, the most aggressive, and the most passionate, the wildest manifestations always

came from Brezhnev. After all, he was the main performer, he was the politician to whom everyone had to adjust, and everyone had to keep to what he, the boss, said. For this reason, don't be surprised if I say that he always stood out as the first and most important person. He was, let me say, the one who stuck most to principle in everything – to use their parlance.

Of course, you don't have to be much of a psychologist to feel what I, for example, felt about Kadar. I don't know why, but in the break I didn't sit beside Ulbricht, nor next to Kosygin, with whom I could have talked in Russian with much greater ease, but instead I saw Kadar, and sat next to him. If someone were to ask: Why did you go over to Kadar? I would reply: I don't know, but somehow I felt that I had to sit there. This is my opinion, and this is how I feel about it now, as you have put this question to me. I saw in him a slightly different person from the others who were there, not only because he had suffered so much in the past, but because I thought that at least with him I could find some kind of understanding, which he would express to the others – except that, for that, a knowledge of the situation at that time was needed. As a young man, I stood somewhere at the head of a party with a certain policy, in defence of which I dared to stand up to this superior force.

And how did your relations with Kadar develop afterwards, after Dresden?

I would like to finish my line of thought. . . . So, I stood up to this great superior force, but I didn't even know what Kadar was going through, what the thoughts in his mind were. I think that, deep down, he sympathized with me, but that was not enough.

44

And after Dresden?

I will carry on, ask me later about the Warsaw matters, for
they are interesting too. Here in Dresden, Kadar did not
act by saying: 'Hang on a minute, the Czechoslovaks have
developed some kind of policy, let's hear them out as to
what they want to do, and how, for they have some kind of
goal; what can their plan be?' He should have done something
like that. You know the fear or obedience which they had
developed . . . if the CPSU leadership said something, you
had to agree with it down to the last word; it was necessary
to put unconditional trust in them, and everything had to
happen according to their instructions. This was the custom.
And here, something appeared that diverged from this custom.
They immediately told us: 'You are withdrawing from the
principles of co-operation and internationalism.' But this was
not true.

You went to Budapest, at Kadar's invitation, the same year.
How did your personal relations with Kadar continue to
develop?

To tell you the truth, I thought Kadar was very near to me,
I considered him very close. And, naturally this manifested
itself also in that . . . you are talking of 1968 now, when I
was in Budapest?

Yes.

At that time, I was in your country at the head of a party
and government delegation, to finalize and sign a treaty of
friendship, co-operation and mutual military assistance. For
ultimately, we are close neighbours, or as you say: [he says
these words in Hungarian] 'We are neighbours, aren't we?'
So, with this treaty we strengthened our friendship. This was
our view of the future: since we were linked to our southern
neighbours, the Hungarians, by the revolutionary past, future

45

developments would also take shape in a spirit of co-operation. Now, as you know, the result was not good.

Did he not give you advice? For example: 'Look here, Comrade Dubcek, you have good intentions. We too would like reforms in the economy. Why don't you act a little more discreetly with the Russians. Perhaps this could also be done differently . . .?'
Did he not give you advice, as an older man?
In conversation with him, he mostly told me that this or that kind of thing should not be published in the press. So that they could not say that we had staged some kind of onslaught on the Soviet leadership. But, you must understand, when we began to work on the Action Programme, what was the one thing which, according to the Soviets, I could then have done and which they would have expected of me? That I should put a brake on it, that I should take stronger action, that I should put a stop to it?

Put everyone in prison?
That's it. . . So, if I can put it this way: I was the father who gave birth to the idea of reform, although many people dispute this today. They try to reduce my role, as if all this were a lie. At the same time, I was expected to dig the grave for what I – naturally together with my associates – had endeavoured to create. I was not the slightest bit aggressive vis-à-vis the Soviet leadership. I always took action only to enable us to gain adequate scope to implement this new policy. But you must understand one thing: neither Kadar nor any of the others were willing to discuss how we wanted to reform the economy or what kind of enterprise law we had elaborated. No!

Instead, they brought a pile of newspaper cuttings and Brezhnev and the others looked at the articles, and then they said: 'What is this for? And why has this organization been formed? And do you know that X or Y has spoken out against the party in the K-231 Club?'

Do you understand? All this is painful; it is painful for me to keep on repeating these things, but I would like you to understand that it was not a matter of our sitting down and discussing, for example, the company law. No, because we could have prepared for that. They deliberately brought up marginal phenomena, to persuade me and the whole party leadership to strike down with our fists, to resist those who acted in a nonconformist way, that is, in a way different from myself and the party leadership.

And in my opinion – I will tell you honestly – without exception, the main intention of the leaders of the five socialist countries, those five who finally met in Warsaw, was to manipulate me so that I should resort to some kind of administrative measures against those nonconformist tendencies. And if I had taken a step of this kind, I would have taken a second one, and a third, and then they would have had me – and they would have been able to force me onto the path which we are already familiar with, which Poland followed after 1969.

For what did Gomulka do? He obeyed! We know the Poles also wanted to implement reforms. They wanted to. But they didn't have any kind of reform programme. And what did they do? They accepted the Brezhnev line, they struck at the universities, just as happened later on in Czechoslovakia. And Gomulka did indeed strike. He shut down the universities, and then came the truncheons. They broke up the teaching staff. In my opinion, they wanted to put me into a similar situation. Their efforts were aimed at making sure that the Action Programme could not be realized. What is more, we probably would not have been allowed even to adopt the Action Programme. As I said earlier, their people must have informed them about the spirit in which this Action Programme was being prepared. So, they dwelt on the least significant matters, they magnified them, blew them up out of all proportion, as if this is where the essence lay. And of course if somebody puts these marginal phenomena all together into a pile, then it becomes a really big pile.

But they took no note of the fact that the people, the party membership, the nation, was supporting the Communist Party and socialism in their actions. They said: this and that is happening. So, everyone, including Kadar, revealed a common characteristic: none of them had enough moral strength to take a stand on my side. But I will answer this with the question relating to Warsaw, for I am sure you will have a question of this kind.

I should like to ask something. It was Ota Sik,* wasn't it, who worked out the economic reform programme. You have been accused, both now and earlier, of allowing yourself to be influenced by this revisionist, this bourgeois economist, Ota Sik. What do you say to this? It is more or less a question of what we Hungarians are doing now – the same reforms.

Something very similar. Well, economic reform is a very serious matter. But our Central Committee, myself included, considered that, as regards the development of Czechoslovakia – and that of the other socialist countries too – the essence of the problem lay not in the economy but in politics. In my view, the main problem was that the sorting out should have been started in the political sphere. Politics then opens the way for economic reforms, for the democratization of society, for pluralistic views, for the press, etc. So for me, it was not the economy, but politics, which was of primary importance. I emphasize this because for many people this was not sufficiently clear.

---

* Ota Sik was an economist who played a leading part in Czechoslovakia's reform programme of 1968. For a brief period in 1968 he was Deputy Prime Minister, responsible for the implementation of the economic reform. After Soviet intervention he went into exile, and is now a professor of economics in Switzerland.

The economic reforms were created in the following way. In my opinion, and not just in my opinion, Sik played an enormous part, partly because, before this, he worked at the Party Academy, and at the Scientific Academy. He was the director of the Academy's Economic Institute. Then he left that sphere, and concentrated solely on economic problems. Naturally, these problems did not become obvious only in the institute; they had been seen much earlier in the factories. The enterprise directors had seen them, as had the Party secretaries, and the communists working in the factories. They saw that something was not right, that our development was not advancing as might have been expected. And although Sik's work in this field is much to be respected, it was not regarded as revisionism, even back in the days of Novotny. For in the Novotny era, when he began to deal with these economic questions, Sik was awarded the Klement Gottwald Order, our highest decoration. But it is not correct to narrow the matter down to just Ota Sik himself. Mention must also be made, for example, of the work of Professor Kadlec, lecturer in Economics at the University, who later also became a Minister; or in Slovakia of Pavlena, Koctuch, and other professors of economics. I can't think of names now on the spur of the moment, but there were several dozen people. If I say that the party needed a political programme, it is clear that an optimal programme had to be worked out which best suited the times, and which would be progressive as well. Thus, we put together in a group all these economists, including Sik, who had the best elaborated answers to these questions, and the whole group worked on the economic reform.

Today, we know that this was seen by the Brezhnev leadership as revisionism. At the beginning, they did not accuse me, or others, of revisionism. This is only today's version, established in the 1970s. They were watching the 'right-wing, anti-socialist forces'. Now, I am this right-wing anti-socialist element! But then, our way of thinking was that there was an Action Programme, and there were people to the left and to the right of it. The Action Programme was the yardstick. But what happened after the military intervention and 1969? The party leadership, hallmarked with the Action Programme, became 'revisionist' and 'opportunist', and so everything was given a different evaluation. This interpretation supports the theory that the marginal phenomena mentioned at Dresden and other talks, were not the point. The main aim they were after was the elimination of the Action Programme, and they succeeded too – but only after 1969.

I believe you were invited, and you were not willing to go to the Warsaw meeting. *

Well, that is not exactly what happened. The way you put the question . . . your wording can be found in many of our publications too, so I am not surprised at your question, but even the starting point of the question is incorrect. We did not refuse to participate. When they invited us to this meeting, it was quite clear to us, after our earlier experiences, that we were to be pilloried. We were not so naive as not to have thought of this. And in this situation, we knew that we had to go there well prepared, so that we should not spend time arguing about who came up with what in the Party, or what kind of article somebody had written, what kind of undesirable article had appeared, but that instead we should evaluate the Party's programme and policies, the official policies. . . . .

* The joint meeting on 14 and 15 July in Warsaw of the leaders of the Communist Parties of the USSR, Poland, Hungary, Bulgaria and East Germany, at which it was decided to send a letter – the so-called Warsaw letter – to the Czechoslovak Communist Party stating that the situation in Czechoslovakia was 'absolutely unacceptable'.

You wanted to put forward arguments. . . .
Of course. Beforehand we had received five letters. Nice and
quietly, we had received five letters: from the Soviet Union,
the Hungarians, the Germans, the Poles, from everyone.
Individual letters. And of course, they then claimed that I
kept these secret, that I did not discuss them with the Party
leadership. Now at last I have the opportunity to declare that
this is a lie. This lie appeared in *Rude Pravo*. The present-day
'marxists' from the Institute of Marxism-Leninism, who are
now in power, write that I concealed this or that. But once
again I declare: I did not hide anything! We discussed these
five letters too. There was a particular nuance to each letter,
there were differences in shades of meaning between them.
And as we saw these differences, we thought: first of all, we
have to conduct bilateral negotiations. This, however, did not
accord with the ideas of the Moscow leadership.

'But then how?' I said. If five letters have arrived, we have
to meet first of all the Hungarians, then the Poles, then the
Germans and so on. We will meet everyone and clarify the
matter, and as the culmination, we will hold a joint meeting. It
should not be the other way round, seeing that I have received
five letters. But you see, I now know what I did not know then:
that time was pressing for them.

Time did not play a part for us, but for them it did. They
were in a hurry. This is why they did not want these bilateral
talks, but they wanted the joint meeting to take place where
they, I don't know. . . .

In practice they would put you on trial?
On trial, yes. . . . so, they wanted the Warsaw letter approved
there. So I said, 'Let's not hold this Warsaw meeting. First let
us hold individual bilateral talks. And only after that should
we all meet? Our reply can be read in our resolutions,
memoranda, in the minutes, in Party documents. We did

not reject the Warsaw meeting. We said, 'Seeing that it is a question of us, and you wish to help us, we are of the view that, first of all, bilateral talks have to be held. Only after that can we all meet.' This was unacceptable to them because as I see it now, they were in a great hurry to prevent the Action Programme from being realized, because they knew, perhaps they already knew then, that the military intervention was under preparation, as I might have suspected. Such thoughts could have sprung into my mind, but they obviously knew in which way they were directing matters; they had some kind of strategy for exerting pressure, some kind of idea of progression, which direction they would drive events, after the military intervention, seeing that they could not have achieved their aim with internal forces.

So we did not reject the invitation, we wanted to go to Warsaw. But, in Warsaw, they approved the letter without us – it can be seen from this too, that they were in a hurry – and sent me this letter. After I received it – I knew already, for they had told me on the phone – we asked them not to make it public. I said: 'It happened, you had a meeting without us. Let us treat this as an internal party matter, let's discuss it within the party, and decide after that, how and in which way we should communicate it.

But no. They had agreed, and in all five countries, in Budapest, in Warsaw . . . they released it. And in Czechoslovakia? – Everyone was asking: the Hungarians, the Germans, etc, everyone was saying: What has happened? I said, 'Let's convene a meeting of the Party Central Committee'. And certain people jumped up: Good God! You know, my friends were saying: 'Don't you understand that Warsaw was to dissolve the leadership of the Czechoslovak Communist Party, to break up the Central Committee of the Czechoslovak Communist Party, to divide it, to incite the members one against the other, and in this way to hinder the Party's present policies?'

They said that to convene the Central Committee would be dangerous, for this Central Committee was still the one put together by Novotny. But I said: 'The Central Committee is the highest organ of the Party. The Central Committee must be convened.' Many people clutched their heads: 'We are convening the Central Committee in such a situation? This is exactly the moment when the dogmatists, the Stalinists will raise their heads.' I replied: 'Let them!'

We convened the Central Committee [on 19 July] and made the letter known. We debated it first of all in the Presidium, then in the Central Committee plenum. The Central Committee plenum adopted a stand too. If the Central Committee was strong enough to get from October 1967, through December, to January 1968, to the working out of the Action Programme, then it had to be strong enough to decide in a just way what kind of stand it was to adopt in connection with the decision of the five communist parties in Warsaw. And so it turned out. So, what did we do? Seeing that they had published the Warsaw letter, we too made it public, but we also publicized our position. And we demanded that they publicize also to their communists, to their people, what we were saying. And my reply was there too, in which I insisted that it be said publicly: the Party's Central Committee has decided definitively, and that is our stance.

But they did not publish this?
No, they did not. The closing lines of our reply read as follows: 'The Central Committee Presidium of the Czechoslovak Communist Party has the task (we determined this task at the plenum) to do everything in the interest of putting to rights relations with the communist parties which met at Warsaw.' There you are!

One moment. At this Central Committee plenum, did people like Indra, Kolder, or even Husak,* people who would later become your opponents, support the Brezhnev line? Bilak and so on? Did anybody defend this standpoint in your Central Committee?

There were speeches at the Central Committee plenum – for example, from Kolder and others – which were worded in a much sharper way than others, and drew attention to the same things which Brezhnev, for example, also mentioned. But, I repeat: it was not these things which were at stake in the given political game! It was a question of completely different things in the political game. Of course on the surface it appeared to be a question of the other, but in truth, the battle was directed at the content.

Did Tito give you any kind of advice at this time?

Well, if not exactly advice, he was very well received here in Czechoslovakia. In my opinion, he did not expect military

---

* Alois Indra is a hardline Communist who opposed Dubcek's reforms and was said to have been behind the 'invitation' of Soviet troops to Czechoslovakia. He was to head the new revolutionary worker-peasant government. Later he became the Speaker of the Czechoslovak parliament but was forced to resign at the end of 1989, and was subsequently stripped of his Party membership.

Drahomir Kolder was also a leading hardline Communist who opposed Dubcek's reforms. He died in 1972.

Gustav Husak was a prominent Slovak-born Communist who played a prominent role in the anti-fascist resistence struggle and in Slovak affairs. He held numerous Slovak government posts before his arrest in 1951 on trumped up charges of 'bourgeois [i.e. Slovak] nationalism'. He was expelled from the Party and in 1954 sentenced to life imprisonment. Released in 1960 and rehabilitated he went on to succeed Dubcek in April 1969 as the First Party Secretary, and was later elected Czechoslovak President. He presided over widespread purges of reform-minded Communists and reversed the reform policies instituted by Dubcek. He pursued a hardline policy for 22 years, and is held responsible for the country's stagnation. After student demonstrations in November 1989 he resigned his Party posts and was subsequently expelled from the Party. At the end of 1989 he was succeeded as Czechoslovak President by Vaclav Havel.

intervention either. You know, to a politician, it is a complete impossibility . . . so it cannot be taken amiss if one did not even try to imagine that the answer would be a military solution. I did not reckon that there would be a military intervention, and nor did Tito. Except that of course he had had experience, he knew them. But then I knew them too! And perhaps better. I knew the way of life there, the work there. Furthermore, in my youth I attended a Soviet school, and I had insight into the so-called contemporary, modern problems of socialism. In other words, I did not feel myself to be as naive as I am often considered to have been; they portray me as if I did not know how and what to do in politics. But there was no question of Tito having warned us directly about anything. Rather, he spoke about the fact that he did not like this or that marginal phenomenon, secondary matter, which clashed with our official policy. He said something ought to be done about it. This was natural. And we – what did we do? We held active meetings; I called together the chief editors, and then the Central Committee Secretaries called them together too, and we told them: 'You yourselves have to pay attention to self-censorship.'

At that time, we took certain measures. For example, in the government we approved certain fundamental principles – in foreign policy and other areas – which could not be disputed, which corresponded to the interests of state policy, etc. We introduced several such measures to restrict articles which were harmful to the renewal which was by now under way. For, looking at it objectively, it really seemed as if these articles had been written to order. Then they plucked them out and argued against us on the basis of the articles. The articles only distracted attention. If the leaders had used sufficiently professional and able self-censorship in certain editorials, if they had been up to their task, they themselves would have put a stop to the over-shrill voices, for they would have seen that our opponents were making use of all this against the party leadership, against the state leadership, and that the articles were distracting attention away from the essence of the matter. So, it was in our interest to put a limit to these manifestations, and we took steps in this direction. But we took the kind of measures whereby nobody was put behind bars, nothing was dissolved. All that was said was: 'It won't do like this, don't publish this, you should co-ordinate this with our standpoint so that you don't damage foreign policy relations, etc. You have the Warsaw Treaty, which is untouchable. Our government, our country, the Party Central Committee will not change anything in connection with this. Don't touch this.' Some people once organized some kind of conference somewhere, and invited a head of department from Party headquarters who said something about our relations with the Warsaw Treaty which did not accord with the instructions of the time. We had to replace him. We had to; it was logical, because he had touched upon things that we wanted to adhere to in politics, in order to gain at least a minimum room for manoeuvre, so that we would be able to implement our internal policy which would advance economic reform. This is why we did not want to change anything in our foreign policy relations.

I told Kadar and also Tito, and the others, that we would curb these extremes, for I myself also felt that they were working against us. However, if you examine these matters now – oh my God! How insignificant they were compared to the glory of God! And for me, the glory of God was the nation, the movement – that was everything! Later, they highlighted, and emphasized extremely marginal phenomena. For as they say in our country: 'He who wants to beat a dog, will always find a stick.' Unfortunately this is what happened. We took measures, but look what finally happened . . .

You didn't expect that?
We did think about it, as I have said, but I did not believe it would happen, for I considered it to be such an extreme solution that it would be a catastrophe not only for us but for the whole of socialism. So, I did not think it would happen.

We shall talk about August too. What did Ceausescu say to you around that time? In the summer of 1968?
We came to an understanding with Ceausescu, with Romania. Our relations with Ceausescu – from the point of view of the interpretation of internal problems – were free from conflict. At that time, Ceausescu held very strongly to one thing, not just in the talks, but in political practice too; he stated that all this was the internal affair of the Czechoslovak Communist Party. This stance was characteristic of our later talks too, when he visited our country.* We made an agreement, everything was very impressive, he had a good reception. So all I can add is that he kept to this policy, this stance of his, in contrast to others who did not behave in such a way. I say this because I was very disappointed (of course, you said we would go on to talk about this, and perhaps when we do, I will say more about it), but as it has come to mind now, I will say it. I thought it would be Kadar who would say no. That he would say 'It cannot be'. Or that Gomulka would find sufficient strength in himself. This is what I was expecting rather.

Was this a personal disappointment to you?
I had the feeling that if this solution were really to come up, then first of all somebody would say: 'Wait a minute, what are we going to do?' or that they would openly oppose the CPSU

---

*President Ceausescu visited Prague on a state visit on 15–16 August and a treaty of friendship was signed.

leadership of the time, that they would not provide an army, not provide soldiers, for we were also members of the Warsaw Pact. Czechoslovakia is a member of the Warsaw Pact. The Warsaw Pact cannot pass any resolution; it cannot launch a campaign against a socialist country without that country's approval. For this reason, I thought this would not happen. So this is why I say, as you have asked about Ceausescu, that I acknowledged then, and I acknowledge today also, that at that time, Ceausescu found enough strength in himself to say no. And for this reason, they did not invite him to these meetings, because . . . obviously they would have had to consult with him. From what I discerned, he was not such a naive politician either, as not to realize what kind of turn events were taking. And it is also very important that he did not really approve of our internal political development. Nevertheless, he said: 'This is the internal affair of the Czechoslovak Communist Party.' Later on, therefore, he was excluded from the meetings because, in my opinion – but this really is only my opinion, for I did not have the opportunity to meet him afterwards; there was no opportunity for the two of us to have a chat – he rejected this radical intervention into the life of Czechoslovakia and into our process of renewal.

[It is perhaps clear by now – mainly from my memories of the 1968 Bratislava 'entry' – that the reporter in this interview from the start deplored, moreover condemned and was deeply ashamed of, the 'tank outing'. One of the attractive features of the Kadar era was that anyone who did not agree with 'giving internationalist aid' – and it is no secret that the Hungarian people, and furthermore a large part of the party membership, was in this category then and also today – was not obliged to take a public stand, to make a declaration of loyalty. Admittedly, it was not advisable for those working in the political sphere to voice their opposition very forcefully or openly, either.

Andras Tompe, the veteran communist who in 1968 was Hungary's Ambassador in Berlin, expressed his disapproval in a letter. He was recalled, and soon placed elsewhere. They tolerated the unworthy persecution launched against him in his new job, as a consequence of which Tompe seized a gun and voluntarily left this life. We journalists, however, could even allow ourselves the luxury of making mocking jokes over the years, about the 'heroic' military action . . . (For example: Where are you going on holiday? Answer: To Czechoslovakia, by tank.)

Of course, theories abounded in Hungary when Janos Kadar made no public appearances from August to October 1968 – up to the time of the swift recall of the Hungarian troops – as if he wanted to convey the impression that he had agreed to the participation of Hungarian troops against his own convictions. It was for this reason that I asked about this in the interview. (Later, *Rude Pravo* wrote on this subject that Dubcek had slandered Kadar!)]

Allow me to ask a question in order to test out a theory. It is said in Hungary that Janos Kadar could have said no to the intervention in Czechoslovakia, saying to Brezhnev, 'Comrade Brezhnev, we support you in principle, only since there are 700,000 Magyars living in southern Slovakia, we are linked by a particular special relationship to Czechoslovakia. For this reason, we cannot send in soldiers.' But, according to the theory, Janos Kadar feared for his own reform plans and for his plans related to maintaining an independent Hungarian internal policy. Supposedly that is why he took part in the end, together with the other four Warsaw Pact member countries, in the military intervention. But he did so very reluctantly, and two months later, in October he was the first to withdraw Hungarian troops from Slovakia. What do you say to this theory?

I believe it is not possible to agree with your theory that in practice Kadar might have wanted, by this means, to protect some kind of Hungarian reforms. In my opinion, it was by agreeing to the intervention that he buried the Hungarian reforms, because the deed is the essence – not what one thinks, but the effect one's deeds generate. The reform movement came to a halt, not only in Czechoslovakia, but in the Soviet Union and in Hungary too, for twenty years because of this.

For in Hungary, what kind of reform movement was it? Some kind of comprehensive political reform programme – as far as I could learn anything about it from here and there in the press (for in our country not everything is written about Hungary, since you are also considered revisionists). If I project this back to the year 1968 then you are revisionists to an increased extent. However, I don't want to offend the Hungarian leadership. But if I look at the dimensions, the arithmetic, and if I take into account the labels attached at the Warsaw meeting, then there are now super-revisionists in Hungary! Why am I mentioning this? In my view, Kadar and Gomulka ought to have done everything in their power; they were the only ones who could have prevented this step. In that case, the situation would have looked like this: Czechoslovakia, Hungary, Poland, no matter how we take it, Romania too, would have stood on the same side. Not to mention Yugoslavia. For, in connection with Warsaw, we proposed that there should be a consultation, yes, but that we should also invite the Yugoslavs, since Yugoslavia was also a socialist country. Or perhaps not? What a great difference it would have made if, from amongst the other countries, others had said no. At the time, I did not even know what kind of letter the French or the Italians had sent to Brezhnev, saying: 'We do not agree, and we cannot support your demands.' I only found out about it later. And if Kadar or someone else had said the same? You say that Kadar was protecting Hungary, but what did he protect? The preservation of the Brezhnev system. Was it necessary for Hungary to preserve the Brezhnev system? No, that is not what Hungary needed. In my view, it needed to protect the reform movement in Czechoslovakia so that perhaps things in Hungary would have moved forward too. However, what happened hampered the whole thing.

What would have happened if Kadar had said 'It cannot be!'
In my view, he would have put Brezhnev in a very difficult position.

But Brezhnev could have removed Kadar from one day to the next.
It's easy to say that. In my view, Kadar's position in the leadership of the Hungarian Communist Party was such that he would not have been able to carry through this removal in the Central Committee.

And Gomulka? . . .
He would not have managed it because, you see, the Central Committee of which I was First Secretary was put together in the Congresses before I took up this position. Think about it, about how strong it was when it came to the battle for ideas! And in my opinion, in the Hungarian Central Committee too . . . for it was this Central Committee which would have had to remove Kadar. In my opinion, Kadar had no grounds for anxiety, for this Central Committee constituted an absolute support for him. Intervention? We were not in 1956 now! In my opinion this was absurd, such an idea was utterly precluded. And without the Hungarian army? What would have happened if Hungarian troops had not crossed the

Czechoslovak border? Would the Bulgarian army and the Germans have turned against Budapest? In my opinion this was not feasible. I don't know . . .

I don't want to be unjust, but I think this was a great political mistake. Life has proved that Kadar's assent to the Hungarian army taking part in the intervention was a mistake; his intervention on 'moral' grounds into the good neighbourly relations we had with Hungary was an enormous political mistake. It had a bad effect on these good neighbourly relations. It was all the same, whether the soldiers were here for one day, two days, three days, or two weeks. They came into this country, they occupied a part of this territory, and unfortunately the tragedy is that they occupied precisely that territory which was occupied when the first Czechoslovak Republic was overthrown [in 1938]. And for Czechoslovakia, this left a very bitter taste. For, when they overthrew the republic, – as you well know – the territory from Bratislava to Kosice was chopped off. And when, again, the Hungarians came along that same line to 'liberate' Czechoslovakia, well you must admit . . . This can only be understood if you talk to the Hungarians living here, as I have talked to them, those who are very close to me, and to whom I feel very close. They did not welcome the Hungarian army. This is the great thing. The Hungarian population accepted our movement for renewal. The Hungarians did not, either then or now – you can ask them – like the intervention. Of course, they restrained themselves, for in the final analysis it was after all Hungarians who came in, but I think they would have given anything for the Hungarian army not to have come then.

I remember Gyula Lorincz* saying he was on very good terms with you, and neither you nor he expected. . . .
Lorincz? He was in the committee which expelled me from the Party.

But that was later.
Yes, later.

But in August, like you, he did not expect the military intervention. . . .
This is hard to tell now. At the end of his career, Lorincz belonged to the Bilak group. Earlier, I too did not know the things about Bilak which I now know. It is easy to be wise after the event. Now, many people say: 'Didn't you know?!'

So, events led up to Cierna nad Tisou.† You sat in that railway carriage face to face with Brezhnev, Podgorny and the others. Was it possible by then to detect that the mutual relationship had deteriorated irrevocably, or not yet?
I would say the following. When the meeting at Cierna nad Tisou took place, it was one on which I had also insisted, and also that the Central Committee plenum should oblige the Presidium to do everything in its power so that relations should not deteriorate; and that it should settle its relations with those communist parties which had accepted the Warsaw letter. If they now agreed that the leaderships of the CPCZ and the CPSU should have talks with each other within the framework of a bilateral meeting, then I welcomed this, for it

---

*The late Julius (the Slovak equivalent of Gyula) Lorincz was a Hungarian-speaking minor politician active mainly in Slovakia . He was at one time the chairman of the Hungarian Citizens Cultural Association in Czechoslovakia and the Chief Editor of the Hungarian language newspaper *Uj Szo* published in Czechoslovakia.

†The Czechoslovak and Soviet leaders met at Cierna nad Tisou near the Russian border from 29 July to 1 August.

63

was in harmony with our earlier proposal.

There is only one thing in connection with this story which I think is distorted to this day. I think Bilak wrote this somewhere too. That is, what kind of relations I could have had with the Soviet leadership, if I sat down to have talks with them in an ordinary railway carriage. But it was not I who determined European and world politics at that time, but Brezhnev and the other high-handed people. What power! Just think, could I have said at that time that we should hold talks in a railway carriage?

So who proposed this strange place?
It was their idea. I went there, and I said: 'Let's go to Kosice at least'. This is a difficult point . . . history must clarify the reasons.

I wonder why they didn't want to go into Kosice?
It is hard to guess why. One can only suppose that perhaps they wanted to be close to their own frontier, in case they felt caught.

Was it their own carriage, a Soviet railway carriage?
They came in their own carriage, and went back again to the carriage which they had come in, for the night. They didn't even sleep on our side of the border. Of course, this was an impossible procedure. So not only was it they who didn't want to go to Kosice, . . . it is now I who am accused; why did I propose this solution, namely, Cierna nad Tisou? But it was not I, it was they who proposed the village, and that we should go there in railway carriages.

Perhaps they were afraid of meeting the Czechoslovak population?
I think that, already then, they were up to no good. It is

possible that, even then, they were contemplating military intervention.

The general staff were obviously well into planning things by that time. I remember that on 3 August, there was a big joint meeting of Communist Party leaders in Bratislava, a large meeting, in a very pleasant atmosphere, although by then the general staffs were preparing plans for storming Czechoslovakia. And at the same time, here in the Bratislava Slavin, here on the hill where we are now sitting, you all talked and said farewell in a friendly atmosphere to Brezhnev, Kadar and the other leaders. How did this happen?

To explain this you have to go back to Cierna nad Tisou. If you have the opportunity, read the communiqué. You know, we on the Czechoslovak side did not have such superiority that we could have proposed the text of the communiqué. It was not as if it were the leaders of two independent communist parties who were meeting each other. So, at Cierna nad Tisou, when the talks ended, the Soviet side worded this draft communiqué.

And you signed it?

The communiqué? We took cognizance of it. It is not usual to sign, only to take cognizance . . . It simply said that a meeting had been held. . . . But the truth is as follows. When we were holding the talks, not just in the carriage, but in the Railway Workers Cultural Centre, their Presidium on the one side, we on the other, there was nothing in common in our avowed political views on fundamental questions! They took one stance, and I took a different stance. So no kind of document could be drawn up which we would have approved and which would have patched up the bad results of the Warsaw meeting. When I went to the meeting, I naturally had to think of some sort of solution which would not lead back to

Warsaw and which did not strengthen the Warsaw resolution. I could not have done that to this nation, even if it had cost me my life. I could not have become the gravedigger of our newly formed politics. Therefore, I had to explain, patiently, what the truth was.

I said, 'We have a new programme, which is followed by the entire Party. The whole nation is following it, everybody, Czechs, Slovaks, the Hungarians, the Ukrainians living in our country. This is spontaneous support. Although there are peripheral demonstrations, the Party now enjoys a prestige which it has perhaps never before enjoyed in history. People are joining the Party in their thousands. People are collecting for the Republic Fund now. I don't even know what this is. It had to be examined in the bank, what this fund was. They didn't even know in the bank what this was all about, where they should put all this money. People are taking money into the banks, gold and everything, watches, rings. The bank directors and the Finance Minister asked what they should do with it. I said, open a current account. The nation is moving. There is an all-national solution. Please, don't compare us to 1956 in Hungary! A counter-revolution? There is no counter-revolution in our country! I am only telling you what is happening in Czechoslovakia: here, not one agricultural producers' co-operative has been dissolved, here workers are working without any dilly-dallying. The work performances are getting much better and higher. The Party enjoys such a measure of prestige. The people, the intellectuals, everybody supports the Party. The extreme cases, for example that here or there people have stood up against the Communist Party, against something elsewhere, that somewhere else an anti-Soviet article has been published in a newspaper ... these are peripheral manifestations and they will fall by the wayside of their own accord. The froth will disperse and only the clean water will remain.

I said: 'In politics, only the substance has to be considered. There is no need for any kind of comparisons. There are no internal forces in this country which could overthrow this regime, these policies.' They, of course, again listed all the negative phenomena. Well, what could be done? It can be seen also from what has been said that my line was to tell the truth about what the real situation was, to defend our internal policies, at the same time acknowledging that there were extremist peripheral manifestations. You see, we know now, but we knew then too ... What kind of Marxist would we be if we thought that, in the course of such an enormous, huge movement, certain things which did not accord with the official policy would not rise to the surface? I would say that if somebody is a Marxist, he has to understand that other phenomena, which are non-communist, or which do not comply with the policy of the Party and the state, must also exist. This has to be. This is not accidental, it is a rule of natural law. They have to exist. So if somebody demands that they should not exist, it means that you have to grab a whip. But I cannot agree to that.

So can we say that you were already proclaiming the principle of glasnost?
Yes, and we consistently asserted it too. I spoke up at the meeting, at the plenum, and the Secretaries also spoke up. We fought politically because we knew that the nation, the Party, the people were in agreement. Before I forget it, I will come back to the fact that this was precisely why the military intervention happened. Here, within the country, not only were there no counter-revolutionary forces, there were no forces at all that could have endangered socialism. If something was endangering socialism – we know very well – it was the dogmatism of Brezhnev! This endangered socialism, weakened the position of the Party, weakened the parties of

the international communist movement, social democracy, the left-wing socialist parties. And why? In order to serve a kind of policy which was out of step with the interests of democracy, socialism and the people. This is what it was. And since we represented a different kind of policy, there at the negotiations, we could not accept a document which would have strengthened their Warsaw resolution. So, do you know what they proposed?

What?

Well, it was voiced: since there are differing standpoints, we will not take joint minutes. Of course we had the wherewithal to do this. We had shorthand writers with us. So, I said: all right, if we're not going to do anything, then let's not do anything. I see now how much ill-will there was in that railway carriage.... We then instructed our shorthand writers to collect up all the material, and put it in the archives. Then, some time later, they told me that some kind of minute-book had arrived from Moscow. I was surprised; what kind of minute-book? Our shorthand notes were in the archives; we had said there were to be no minutes. Who had put together a minute-book? Well, apparently the Moscow leadership had put together a minute-book and had sent it on to us afterwards. But this was after the military intervention. I don't remember the exact date.

What I am trying to say is, the most positive thing in all this was that we said: 'Let there be another meeting. You can see, there are differences of opinion between us. We have to find a common language, and work out a document which will be acceptable to us in the given situation. And, let the Hungarians, Germans, Poles, everyone, take part in this meeting. But,' I said, 'a new document has to be worked out.'

[Here, the fourth cassette ran out. Marton 'Bozso', our

cameraman, got out the fifth. We were now in the middle of the second hour of the interview. Dubcek, who was 68 years old, showed not the slightest trace of fatigue. In the interval, he happily joked away. He had not one cigarette.

The 'plot' ground inexorably on towards the horror: the account of the most horrific experience of Dubcek's life, the night of 20–21 August. I know it is not easy for him to talk about this. As you will see, on several occasions, he stated: 'Let's leave this, it's very hard to talk about it.' But history has no compassion: our subject is now a valuable source. He cannot deprive future generations of the event in which he was the key witness.]

So, after Cierna nad Tisou, on 3 August you all met in Bratislava. What was your impression then; had they shelved the plans for an intervention?

We know now, of course, that they were making preparations against us. But earlier, we did not know, although we might have thought of it, and taken it into account. But neither I nor many others reached the final conclusion that yes, they would march in. Why? Precisely because the most important thing was achieved at Cierna nad Tisou, that we should draw up a new document. Even if it was a small step, this was something positive. It was visible from the manner in which they held talks with us how unreliable, distrustful, hypocritical, and characterless they were. At that time, we emphasized that in its own way it was something positive that we were drawing up – a new document, and moreover at a high level.

By the way, this contained, very briefly but logically, a statement that I must abide by a document which declared that every communist party must itself resolve its own country's problems, and was responsible to its own people, and that the borders of the sovereign states of the socialist Warsaw Pact were inviolable.

69

But I do not want to tell all the history. Believe me, this was rather uncomfortable in the prevailing circumstances. At any rate, in my opinion the whole document would have become worthless, if these stipulations had not been in it in their entirety.

For precisely this reason, our judgement was that this was a positive thing, and this is what we said in the communiqués, and the speeches. After the meeting on the 3rd, I made a speech on television on the 4th. I do not remember exactly, but I opened with something like: 'Esteemed fellow citizens, I have to inform you that an important meeting of representatives of the communist parties has just ended in Bratislava. This meeting accomplished the task which the Central Committee of the Czechoslovak Communist Party set us: that we should do everything to settle relations with the other communist parties. I can announce that we have accomplished this task. We approved this and that document, and I also inform you that we did not sign any other secret document. That which we accepted, we will also make public. The document has no secret clauses, I declare this sincerely, before the people, the nation.'

Why do I remember this? . . . Well, because this was in the document, and as you yourself also inferred in your question, I considered this to be something positive. If I remember correctly, I spoke on the television on 4 August, and the military intervention came on 21 August.

As you said, they were preparing for it well in advance. You see, sometimes you can try everything, but in the end everything was too little for them, and in the end it was only after 1969 that the Czechoslovak issue could be understood, only after 1969 and 1970. Because for them, even the Bratislava agreement was too little, even if it was something positive. But what would they have required? What I talked about at the beginning too: they

wanted to manipulate us so that we would accept the
Gomulka line, that we would not reform things, not carry
out any kind of renewal, any kind of pluralism, any kind of
glasnost ... that we would not abolish supervision of the
press, that the proven policy of 'existing socialism' would
continue. They were the 'existing socialism'; we were not
the existing socialism!

You see, this was not enough either! They progressed step
by step towards their objective. For example, at international
meetings, they quoted from the communiqué, they read
excerpts from the communiqué accepted at Cierna nad
Tisou, that it was absolutely this or that ... 'Hurrah!
The Czechs agreed to everything' ... But the truth was
what I told you about my performance there. And that was
an achievement, that we agreed to hold another meeting.
And we did. I evaluate Bratislava positively too. For we
did not support the Warsaw letter, but worked out a new
document. And this document – I can assert – was useful
to everyone. Firstly, because it went beyond Warsaw, which
was a separatist action, and worked out a common document
of the kind that was needed. Secondly, we could continue
our policy, we ourselves would resolve our problems. In
this republic, during those two weeks, there was no kind
of counter-revolution, and anyway, who would have taken
steps against President Svoboda? I don't want to brag, but
who would have taken steps against me, against Prime
Minister Cernik, or against the leader of the 1945 Prague
uprising, Smrkovsky?* Or against others? The police here?
The army here? Our Czechoslovak army? Or the people's
militia, of which I was commander? So, who would it have

---

* The late Josef Smrkovsky was one of the prominent personalities of the Prague
Spring of 1968. He had previously held various Party and government posts. In 1951
he was sentenced to life imprisonment on trumpted up charges, was released in 1955
and later rehabilitated. He was once again purged in 1970.

been who, taking steps against these people, would have toppled the socialist system? This was a huge lie, completely unacceptable.

How did the news reach you that foreign troops had set foot on Czechoslovak soil? Were you at home?
I was not at home, I was in the Central Committee building, sitting at my desk.

Late at night?
At night. As the world knows, we put together the text of this appeal . . . In my opinion, they did not expect us to formulate any kind of resolution; they expected that we would fall on our knees, that, for fear of our lives, or something similar, we would be quiet.

But at what time did you find out?
It was at night, late at night. I cannot tell you the exact time now. A minister called me, and Premier Cernik also phoned. It was necessary to verify whether it was true or not, so it was late at night.

By that time they had occupied Ruzyne airport. But can I ask you also about your personal impressions?
We passed a resolution declaring the whole thing unlawful, contrary to all the documents, contrary to our international relations, stating that nobody had called them in.
. . . In the United States, the Soviet Ambassador had already handed over a note addressed to the US President, stating that somebody had called them in. In later publications, this is what they referred to: this invitation, although we had already that night announced on the radio that nobody had called them in, neither the President of the Republic, nor the First Secretary, nor the President of the National Assembly,

nor the President of the National Front. Indeed, from these institutions there was no one who endorsed this, and nothing of this kind was made public. This slowed down the action. We remained in the Central Committee building, and as is customary at such times in civilized states, we waited for somebody to come and . . .

Hand over a note?
Yes, we expected that someone would come who was authorized to say something to the First Secretary or to the Premier. This did not happen. But then in the end they did come, to arrest us.

Soldiers?
Yes. Soldiers.

Armed Soviet soldiers?
Yes. But these are very unpleasant memories.

Nevertheless: Two, three? How many were there?
How many were there? Eight or ten . . .

Did they break straight into your study?
Yes, into my study. One of them pointed a gun at me, tore out the telephone and said: 'Remain seated'. So we waited. Then along came our state security boys too. Well, should I fight them? There was no sense in that. First came Smrkovsky, the President of the Parliament, then Kriegel, the President of the National Front. Then they were led away separately to different places. I was arrested on behalf of the revolutionary court, the revolutionary government. I said to them: 'What is this, who is leading this revolutionary government?' Well, Alois Indra was the answer.

Who appointed him?

Who? Well, not the nation, that's for sure. So, you can see how these things developed, how they took up these positions. There is no precedent for this, and I don't want to talk about these things too much. They touch emotions deeply, they are tragic, not just in a personal sense, but in the revolutionary movement too. They influence our relations with the Soviet Union, and as regards all that happened there or here, well, one tolerates it with difficulty. I do not like to talk about it, but as you have asked me, I have to say something.

They took you, Svoboda, Cernik, Smrkovsky and Kriegel to Moscow, did they not?

What would the coming minutes or hours bring? That was what I was thinking. Something had to happen. If they arrest the First Secretary of the Czechoslovak Communist Party, and the Premier and the President of the Republic, everyone would know that they were not taking them on holiday, especially if this happened in the name of some revolutionary government or revolutionary court. It is obvious that a 'revolutionary court' does not want just to have a chat. We did know that much. But when we had been at the airport for a long time, and I was sitting in that armoured car, and half an hour had gone by, then an hour, then another, a third, and nothing ... and night came and still nothing happened, what we were expecting did not happen ... Well, where do they usually take people at such times? I will not talk about it; you can imagine it. When nothing happened, we thought and thought, what on earth can be happening here? Either the revolutionary government or the revolutionary court which should have carried out something did not exist. There is something, but what is happening? It is night now, a day has gone past, and we're still here. We are still on our home territory, and we thought that if they wanted to do something to us, then they would take us somewhere, somewhere else, that is, that they would not do these kinds of things on one's home territory. But, look, I lived through the war, and I am not the kind of person whose legs would have started quaking at this kind of thing. It was hard. Particularly from a moral point of view, it was a very hard thing. But I am a man who has seen his friend die, who has lived through the war, who lost his brother; I too was injured twice, seriously, but I am still here, and giving you an interview. I have lived through many things.

Where were you injured?
Around the chest and in the leg. First around the chest, but this was a slighter injury, I still managed to escape with this. The second time, they caught me on the leg. But they got my brother in such a way that he died of his injuries (on 22 January 1945). I only wanted to say that when a person gets into this kind of situation, even then he must behave in an unwavering way, because he is fighting for a just cause, and then it is easier to look even a gun in the face, as I did too, when I was arrested, or when I was sitting in that armed transport carrier in which they took me away. For we know from history too that people can endure bad or even the worst things.

You know, they have already asked me about these things once before, in the interview I gave to 'Unita',* Comrade Foa

*Dubcek gave an interview to the Italian Communist daily 'Unita' on 11 January 1988 to mark the twentieth anniversary of his coming to power and the beginning of the Prague Spring. In the article he expressed his sympathy and hope for Gorbachev's programme of perestroika in the USSR, and defended the 1968 reform programme in Czechoslovakia.

asked which moment in my life I viewed as the most critical, the hardest to bear. I have only one answer to this: don't expect an answer to this question from me. Period. I have said what I have said, but I would not like to return to this subject.

I understand that this is difficult for you . . .
No, I am over it now . . . A person prefers to think of the future, of the good things, rather than to think back to the bad things. And the blank spots must be eliminated so that we can advance development. But unfortunately, if these things also happen, then the truth must be told, but not so that we should go back to the past, quite the contrary, so that it should not be repeated; so that things should progress forward, so that the fog should be lifted, for here it is not a question of me, even if they talk about me too, it is a question of those 468,000 communists whom they expelled . . .

How did they take you to Moscow? When did you first meet members of the Czechoslovak delegation again?
My answer is the following: they did not take me and the others to Moscow.

Then to which town?
In the night-time, the following night, they took us, and not very far. There was building work going on which was still not completed. We saw the power shovels, with which the soil was obviously removed, when we passed by them during the night, and then they took us to some wooden hut in Poland. A few other things come to mind, but I shall not mention these because at the moment I don't want to talk about it.

In the end, when did you return to the delegation?
Later, we were taken to Poland, somewhere in the mountains
. . . perhaps somewhere near sub-Carpathia, and we were
there until we were summoned. At first I was the one who was
summoned. A member of the KGB was responsible for me.
Well, he came and said that there had been instructions from
the county party committee that I should go to the telephone.

Which county was it?
It was Uzhgorod . . . probably Uzhgorod . . . Then they gave
me spectacles, probably so that I should not be recognized.
Well, there I was at the telephone and speaking on the line
was Podgorny, who at the time was Chairman of the Supreme
Soviet Presidium.

The Head of State . . .
Yes, and he said that on behalf of the top Soviet leadership
he proposed that I should fly to Moscow to hold talks. I
imagine that we were being listened in on, that every word
was being recorded. We were not in a panic, only cautious,
so that it was safe for them to listen in on our conversations.
Well, by way of reply I asked how would I get there, how
would I get to Moscow to meet the leaders. I asked who
would be there and where the others were, since several of
us had been arrested, some, even, who were not here. In the
end, I said that I wanted to go back to the place I had been
dragged away from. I would not go to Moscow alone – that
was my resolute decision. I would not go, I would stay here.
And in what capacity would they hold talks with me anyway,
as a prisoner or as whom? To this he said: *nu, sto vu, sto vu* –
that is, 'Come on, what do you imagine?'
At this point he began again: 'Well, you could still do this.' I
said: 'If the others don't come, I shall not go anywhere either,'
and I ended the conversation. Then, they obviously conferred,

they examined the pros and cons, and they obviously needed me, because they assented to the others coming as well. In the end, we met in Moscow.

President Ludvik Svoboda originally remained in Prague. How, in the end, did he end up at the Moscow negotiating table?

You mention the President of the Republic. Well, look: to lay hands on the President of the Republic, especially on a figure such as Svoboda, would have been to go right over the top. That is part of the reply. The other thing – and this is most important – in my view they needed the President of the Republic in Prague, in order to be able to submit their demand that a revolutionary government be formed, that this 'revolutionary government' should form a 'revolutionary tribunal', which could have decided summarily on our fate, and on arresting 'anti-Soviet and anti-socialist' people.

You mean: to hang them, like Imre Nagy?*

Well, you know, they certainly would not have taken pity on us, as it emerged from their way of speaking. But what would it be necessary for me to specify in this matter?

So this was how the President of the Republic came to be left in Prague. I believe they underestimated him, just as they underestimated me; they underestimated Smrkovsky, and the Presidium; they underestimated the Central Committee; they underestimated our entire Communist Party; they under-estimated the Czechs, the Slovaks, the Magyars, the

---

*Imre Nagy was a leading Hungarian Communist who also held various leading government posts. He was Prime Minister in October 1956 during the Hungarian uprising and played a leading part. After the crushing of the uprising he was given asylum in the Yugoslav Embassy, which he later left following assurances that his safety would be safeguarded. He was later handed over to Soviet authorities, interned in Romania then taken back to Hungary, sentenced to death and executed in 1958. He was recently fully rehabilitated and given a state funeral in 1989.

Ukrainians living in Czechoslovakia. They simply under-estimated everything, and in the awareness of their own size and strength, they thought that everyone would have to knuckle under to them. I believe that they had one picture only of Svoboda – the image of a valiant soldier. They were only familiar with his relationship with the Soviet Army, and his personal relations with Soviet Defence Minister Grechkov, as well as his other personal relationships with many other military leaders, which came about at the time of the formation of the Czechoslovak Army. However, they were not acquainted with him as a person.

I, however, knew him as a private person, too. This was not by chance. In that complex and difficult situation, when I could not sleep at night, I constantly thought, simply, that I must call up Svoboda. This man – at least as I knew him – was an honest person, a man of character. Perhaps as time passes, he can be blamed for many things, especially after 1969. Yet those who condemn him must take into account his permanently and continuously deteriorating health, and his mental and physical decline, too. For a good number of years, he was President of the Republic, and he did not leave the post with me or others. For this reason, he has been much criticized by some people, but not by me. In my view, the decisive thing is what he did, namely, he refused to accept the 'revolutionary government'; so the revolutionary tribunal could not be created either, and in the final analysis the plan he submitted in Moscow proved correct. He said: 'I insist that all the detainees should be allowed to return to Czechoslovakia; only after that will I be willing to fly to Moscow for talks. And I also insist that the others take part in the talks.' So, there could be no creation of a revolutionary government or tribunal, and we were still able to return.

Is it true that Svoboda threatened to commit suicide if you were not treated fairly?

Look, this is more or less well known. Generally, it happened as follows: it happened when the Ambassador went to see him, as Head of State.

Stepan Chervonenko?

Yes, Chervonenko. He, Svoboda, that is, was able to express his disagreement with our failure to return in the following manner: 'What do you expect of me? What can I do? Should I, perhaps, blow my brains out?' And then he demanded that each one of us should be allowed to return to his same position. So this was the determining and decisive step, after which it really was possible for the so-called Moscow 'talks' to begin. Of course, I don't know how events would have turned out if, prior to Svoboda's stand, the Central Committee's standpoint had not come about, which it announced to the entire world, to international forums: namely, that the intervention was unlawful, that no one had called the troops in, that it was a crime, that it was contrary to international law, that it was contrary to the treaties.

So, after this declaration, Svoboda, as Head of State, took a stand in favour of it. At the same time, one can imagine, at least in theory, what might have happened to this country if Novotny had held that position at the time. It is not necessary to go into this in detail. But I believe Hungarian viewers know this, and the Czechoslovaks also find it easy to imagine.

He probably would have had you hung, like Imre Nagy, as we have already mentioned.

It is more or less certain what would have happened to me, but let us not engage in speculation.

Where were the talks held – in the Kremlin?
Yes. I was summoned to the Kremlin, that was where the talks began. Groups were formed, and work began on the documents.

What was the tone of the talks?
Well, I'll tell you. As is always the case, both sides needed some kind of document. Naturally, we also had a sort of proposal for some kind of document.

I'm curious about the human tone of the talks.
That's just what I wanted to explain. So, we put forward our proposal, but it was unacceptable to the Soviet Union. Therefore, talks in working groups were organized, where some kind of compromise, some new kind of document, was worked out. I refused to participate in this. I said that I would not take part in working out any document. My conviction was that if anything needed doing at all, it had to be done at home. Of course, it was logical that we, the supreme leaders, agreed that we could not reaffirm the legitimacy of the intervention, that we could not alter the Central Committee resolution which condemned the illegal military intervention. We could not give our approval to a winding up of the policy of renewal which we had pursued. It was completely clear that we could not assent to a document which would have led to a winding up of the Action Programme, to an annihilation of our policy's guiding principles. Naturally, my views were clear to the others, because I stated them at the unofficial discussions. There were such things, alongside the sessions of the official group which was working out the document. I believe that my views were also clear to the Soviet side. To whom might they have been clearer than to them? Naturally, they had an interest in such views *not* being in the document. But for us, such an omission was entirely unacceptable.

Is it true that Brezhnev's men were unwilling to sit at the same table as Kriegel, the President of the National Front, the hero and veteran of the Spanish Civil War?

Look, this was how it was: all of us were in favour of everyone being present, including Kriegel. Only Kriegel himself, voluntarily and irrespective of everyone else, said that he would not take part in the talks. Then followed the working out of the documents, still without my participation. Of course, the rest of the delegation were well aware of the things which I could in no way whatsoever accept, and at the discussions, at the plenary sessions, they continued to reject any suggestion that the document should pronounce on the most burning issues, the four things I have already spoken about, because this was entirely unacceptable to us. In the end, the part of the delegation which the Presidium had charged with preparing the document said that it could be signed, because these four things were not in it. There were still passages in it, such as one saying that no harm whatsoever should befall the 'internationalists'. Of course, we still didn't know who these internationalists were, since we also were internationalists! Naturally, it also contained a statement that the Party Congress could not be recognized . . .

But I must still go back to your first question, about Svoboda, that his character played a major role in his decision. Antonin Novotny would have decided differently, but since Ludvik Svoboda was President, he decided as he did. If Novotny had been in office, he would have accepted the 'revolutionary government'. Yet, even before this, when we were apprehended, and we did not know what was happening, the delegates of the extraordinary Party Congress met, and moreover in the CKD factory. This is Prague's biggest mechanical engineering works, in the heart of the traditional industrial proletarian district, where a decisive proportion of the working class are to be found. So this was where this congress was held, under the protection of the people's militia, the working class. And it naturally reaffirmed the stand of the Central Committee Presidium, vis-à-vis the illegal military intervention.

The Soviets later declared this Congress illegal and null and void, on the grounds that the Slovak delegates did not get to the CKD Factory. Gustav Husak also accepted this. What is your opinion on this?

Well, not because the Slovaks were not there! This was an excuse – unfortunately referring precisely to the Slovak party – which was used after the military intervention. But it is not worth analysing, because at the time it was not the determining, the decisive thing. What was most important was that we did not assent to the four points which I have already mentioned, and which were unacceptable. And what is their non-recognition of the Congress associated with? True, there were few people there from Slovakia – only a couple of people here and there.

Yet in a different atmosphere this could have been made good, it would have been possible subsequently to call in delegates, or it would have been possible to continue the Congress and further delegates might have come. Well, you know, that congress was entirely unacceptable to those with power. This was one of the key issues, and it became their basic demand. In the end, all those who were there, including Zdenek Mlynar*, assented to signing the Moscow Protocol, but I continued to oppose signing. One reason for this was the Party Congress, but I have to go back somewhat to the

---

* Zdenek Mlynar is a Moscow-trained lawyer and reformist Communist. He was Dubcek's supporter and played a leading part in the reform movement of 1968. He resigned all his posts in November 1968 and later went into exile to live in Vienna.

time when the Moscow document was still only half-prepared, when work was under way and what was to happen in domestic policy had not yet been expounded in any detail. When I discussed this with my comrades, namely, Smrkovsky, whose stand I was well acquainted with (and he was familiar with mine), I said: we must somehow define what kind of domestic policy we are to pursue. And at that time the Czechoslovak side – if I remember rightly, Smrkovsky in person – held talks for a second time with the Soviets, and insisted that domestic policy should be shaped on the basis of the May plenum of the CPCZ. The Central Committee session in May 1968 had reaffirmed the correctness, the continuation, and the irreversibility of the policy formulated in the Action Programme, and it had also rejected sectarian-dogmatic, and – I'm not afraid to use the word – right-wing, opportunist views. At that time, we classified everything which was not in the Action Programme as being a right-wing opportunist view. We interpreted the Action Programme as a formulation of Marxist-Leninist guidelines. We considered it to be the socialist programme of socialist renewal. Therefore, it was renewal, socialist renewal, that is, unequivocally a socialist programme, headed by the Communist Party.

They did not want to, but in the end they accepted this part in the Moscow document. But the Soviet side did not want even to hear about the legality of the Congress. I went to my colleagues and said: 'Look, if I were now to resign from my position as First Secretary, would this help the Party's leadership?' They did not accept this. So I did not resign. The allegation that I gave it up gradually is mistaken, erroneous. No, I only asked whether it would help if someone else were called in; I asked the Presidium to discuss this. It did not happen! At that time we were in Moscow. I told Cernik: 'You, as head of the government, as a member of the Presidium, put forward why it is that I should not take part in this task you are working on here, even if all the other members of the Presidium are brought here from Czechoslovakia. I shall not go back to Czechoslovakia as First Secretary. Submit this to the Presidium, and accept my resignation. I am being put in a moral situation in which I am not certain whether I shall be able to bear signing something which does not accord with my stance, my convictions.'

Naturally, another factor in this was that I did not feel the same restrictions as previously, since these had been dismantled by the May session of the Central Committee, which had reaffirmed the Action Programme and all we had adopted in this connection. I, but not only I, was able to refer to this programme. The only thing was that earlier, when they said I should ask Tito, since he was well acquainted with 'them', I remember well, I said: 'I'm better acquainted with them than Tito. I am one of their kind, I have lived through what the Soviet Union stands for; in me there is much of their characteristics, their good characteristics – the tenacity which characterizes the Russian, the tenacity of the communists who sacrificed their lives for the revolution!'

But the reason I am like this is not so that what happened to Bela Kun, for example, should happen to me. His revolution did not succeed; he was defeated. Where did he seek protection? In the Soviet Union, where in the end they executed him. Naturally, that is not what I consider steadfastness. What they did during the period of Stalinism when they butchered their own cadres is *barbarity*. It used to be said of the French Revolution that a revolution which devours its own children cannot succeed. And that is why socialism could not succeed in the Soviet Union. It could not reap victory because it was founded on misery, on human suffering, on the suffering of people, of nations. However, the Soviet Union was victorious in the struggle against fascism. And starting out from this, the Soviet State developed into a superpower. Unfortunately, however, it had to suffer such setbacks in the area of democracy and morals that one is barely able to contemplate it. But where was I now? . . . You see, I keep on digressing to these things; these are the things that preoccupy me.

We were talking about your resignation.
Well, I said: accept my resignation. And I will come back to the reason why I digressed like that on to the previous thought. If you will allow me. Because I knew them better than did many others. For I did not trust the Moscow Protocol! I don't claim that this document was not one which at the time could be regarded as some kind of healthy limit, which, at that time, though it was a tragedy even so, could have enabled us to reach some kind of compromise solution which could have salvaged at least the minimum for Czechoslovakia. Everybody knew that the maximum was not attainable. But at least the minimum got into the protocol. According to the protocol we would be able to salvage the minimum. But what was this minimum? To keep the Action Programme. So there was a hope that this nadir could be passed, that certain things would become clarified, things would sort themselves out, and there would not be some kind of tragic break in internal politics.

But in spite of all this I still refused to sign. Do you know why? For this precise reason. Because when we went there, in order to sign the protocol, 'they' and everybody else told me: 'After all, now, there are *acceptable things* in it'! There was only one uncertainty: surrounding the legitimacy of the Party Congress. The way this was formulated was that it had not been entirely perfect, that we would be holding the Congress only some time in the future. But otherwise, we kept to the party line which had been decided on; we did not affirm the legality of the military intervention, which, however, they would have expected; we did not abolish the Action Programme; in other words, the main points remained. So that is how it came about that one could not expect any kind of ideal result, but that the minimum could be saved – it was my colleagues who said this.

But let us look at the question of my resignation. The Presidium discussed it and said that no, they would not accept it. And now imagine if you will how much I often suffer because of those so-called adherents of revival, who either here at home or abroad write about me: 'And yet he signed it!' Well, of course I signed, because there was that compromise. The Presidium, on the other hand, did not accept my resignation. What ought I to have done then, at such a decisive historical moment? Let us just consider what I could have given rise to. I was still able to take one or two small steps to bring us closer to what I had in mind; I was able to alleviate the situation; I was able to seek some kind of way out of this complex situation. Afterwards I was able to return home and prevent the destruction of the Party, in order that the minimum I have just been discussing could be retained, could be salvaged. Therefore I asked myself the question: what will you do? Before that, it had been my determined intention not to sign, not at any price. I told them all: I shall return home as a simple citizen; I have finished. Just get the plenum to sanction what you as a Presidium have adopted here. But as the Presidium did not accept this standpoint of mine . . . Do you understand? By now I was following the way I was brought up. At times like this I must not think only of myself; at times like this I just had to think carefully, to make sure that I did not take some even greater, perhaps unconsidered, step. In other words, in my view, it was this stance of mine which helped our delegation, in that the Soviet Union really had no possibility of forcing on to our delegation the most sensitive things: that is to say, that we should agree with the intervention, that we should strike out the Action Programme, or at least that we should reaffirm the Warsaw resolution. For that is what 'they' would have wanted at the very least! So, my stance helped in this.

You faced a terrible dilemma. But, if I may express an opinion, in my view you chose the only correct solution.

. . . I said to myself: what will you do now? Will you not do it? But you must! Let history judge. This case is similar to when they write that, after I received the news from the Minister of Defence that the armies of the Warsaw Pact had marched in, I should have assented to our not allowing them into the country, and we should have fought. I did the opposite. I rang up Cernik and Svoboda. Cernik rang Svoboda, saying that no mistake should be made. Not one shot should be fired from our side. Let them march in, let them just march into the country; you must not touch anyone, you should show no resistance. I am convinced even now that those allegations that I behaved in a cowardly manner are not true. Like Benes who (when the allies had refused to help) resigned, which meant the end of the republic. I too have that much expertise about strategy. I too know that it was the politicians who had decided on marching in – but who was it who had to carry it out? *The soldiers!* And when the soldiers were given this task, in the course of the preparations for the military operation, what would they think of first of all? I had to guess, to estimate. And I had to reckon with their expecting resistance, to be sure. In other words I, as a politician, who had the possibility of deciding, or if not of deciding, then at least of exercising a decisive influence in such an important situation, I decided that we must not do what 'they' expected, now that I had guessed what they wanted.

It would have cost the lives of huge numbers of people.
That is precisely why I said NO! And to this day I believe I
was right. And even now historians still write and speculate:
perhaps they would have taken fright, they would not have
marched in and they would not have caused a tragedy, because
of the international reaction that would have followed . . . But
they would have caused one! I know these people. I say even
now: I know these people very well!

If they had not known me . . . I am thinking of my former
associates now . . . those who live here at home or abroad,
including Bilak and many others also . . . they say I was too
soft, I did not have a concept . . . But then who had any kind
of concept at that time?

So the question was should we sign or should we not sign. I
said, did I not, that I did not trust protocols, that I considered
them as merely a manoeuvre. Well, just think of it, I was
not wrong. My approach at that time was correct: that one
should not trust them. Nevertheless, I could not commit
the historical mistake of not signing. Because that was the
final historical moment when . . . Let us suppose that I had
rigidly refused to do it, that I did not sign. In that case, from
a historical perspective, it could be said: if he had signed,
perhaps the situation would have developed differently. Do
you understand? I had to exhaust all the possibilities. And
when I signed, this meant that I had a last chance to save what
was salvageable. That is why I decided to sign.

However, as a matter of fact, this was the end of the story,
though many things were still to happen in the meantime. In
that period, when I was still sticking to not signing, I had to
take a step, – even in opposition to our Party's Presidium
– a spectacular step which even in the eyes of the Soviet
side would exclude me from among the signatories. They
had already convened the Soviet plenum, the Soviet Party
Presidium: they sat on one side, we sat on the other. Film

cameras, journalists, everything on the table, and what is customary at such times? At such times one only has to pick up a pen and sign. But what happened was that I stood up and I said: 'Not this! Is this the Moscow protocol? All of you know very well that prior to the talks we, too, drew up a document. So at least let the gradualness also be visible, the sequence of gradual steps by which we arrived at this protocol. The document which we prepared back home and which we brought with us *should form a part of this protocol which is to be signed!*' Brezhnev stood up. 'I warned you not to do this. I warned you, I warned you!' he kept on saying. In the meantime I had sat down.

And then they quickly drove away the reporters and the TV people. Then Brezhnev and the entire Soviet Presidium marched out – and there was no signing. This happened at the time when I was still clinging to my idea that I would not return home as First Secretary. Then one, then another, then a third – I am now speaking of friends, like Smrkovsky, Spacek,* who was my friend and still is, Cernik, the Prime Minister, Simon, the Leading Secretary of Prague and many others – they all said: 'We shouldn't be too hasty; there were, after all, things in the document that we could accept.' And just think, for all that I had broken up an official session. Do you know what that means? Who else, after me, will do such a thing again?

There is no precedent for such a thing.
And then they asked why I hadn't wanted to sign. Because – I say – because I don't trust them. I can't say that here. I'm not even in office now. Where can I say all this? In a letter, giving the reasons why I did not want to sign the Moscow protocol. This was the reason: because I did not trust them.

---

* Josef Spacek, a reformist Communist, Dubcek supporter and member of the Party leadership in 1968 was expelled from the Party in 1970.

Twenty years later I can establish that indeed I was not wrong. Nevertheless I *had* to take this historic step! To provide even the last chance, so that later they should not be able to accuse me of having let an opportunity slip by which might still have salvaged something.

But I know 'them'! So, I considered every circumstance. Compared to the original draft document, this new version already included the Action Programme and, moreover, in harmony with the May plenum. This was the essential thing from the domestic political point of view, and for me it was the decisive thing. So then, together with the others . . . that is to say, it's a kind of training, if the Presidium says don't do it, it can't be otherwise; you feel the responsibility. So, I signed, together with the others. My responsibility was greater than that of Kriegel, who did not sign. I don't want to judge his decision, it was a matter of conscience. I cannot conceive of another way out, and at that time neither could anyone else – not Smrkovsky, nor anyone else. For by then the Protocol did not contain the four points of capitulation; on the other hand, it contained things which indicated a certain positive way out of the difficult situation. And I had to decide in favour of what was more acceptable for the Party and the nation.

In the second phase, after conversing with the members of the Presidium, I no longer insisted on not signing. The question arose in my mind: what if I am wrong? What if, after all, this is the way out? That is why, when I returned home, I set about putting all this into practice. One of my first decisions was to summon Silhan, who had been Leading Secretary during my absence. Our meeting was almost touching. And, naturally, neither of us was light of heart. This is what had been accepted; what could one do? And I still had not told anyone at that time what I was going to do. Only, before I left Moscow, I said to Brezhnev: 'Look, we have declared our last Congress invalid', alleging as the reason the fact that the nationalities were not represented in adequate proportions, etc. But it makes no difference, the reason given is incidental. Right. But I had to take into the Central Committee those whom the Congress had elected and who were still not Central Committee members. You know, in politics, from time to time one had to do things which 'they' did not like. Well, they didn't like this either! But if I am moving towards a goal, then I follow my own line; it is always like that in politics.

Having returned home, we convened the plenum; I convened the Secretaries. I said that from every county delegation we would have to take eight to eleven people. In other words, not two or three, but altogether some 70 people. In other words this corresponded to 50 per cent of the Central Committee. This was one of our first tasks. These people had to be co-opted onto the Central Committee. By this I wanted to make up a little bit for the fact that our Congress could not be recognized. In the Central Committee a political situation evolved such that, since it had not been possible up to the moment of the military intervention to eliminate the new reform policy, *there was no means of doing this even after* the military intervention, if we kept to the principle of the unity of the Party Presidium.

But it soon transpired – tell me if I am wrong – that this unity was beginning to break up within the Central Committee of the CPCZ. And quite soon they managed – by making use of Gustav Husak and others – to remove you from the post you had held up till then and to send you to Ankara, as Ambassador to Turkey. How did this process of erosion take place? Whose infamy or malice speeded up this process?

I mentioned earlier that when they marched in I asked the Presidium whether it would help if someone else were to hold the talks, since in theory one could rightly suppose that they would not be willing to talk with me, having arrested me, isn't that so? But maybe – I thought – they would be willing to talk with someone else. The Presidium did not accept this solution. Now, how did it happen that I left my post? This is also why I now dwell on this point. Because, after all, I could scarcely expect of the Soviet Union and the Soviet leadership, or in practice of any of the five countries that marched in that I should receive an invitation for a visit as First Secretary. So, an absolute blockade developed against me. Objectively, then, in the course of implementing the resolution of the November plenum* (we worked out this resolution on the basis of the Moscow Protocol, and after the participants of the CKD Congress had been co-opted onto the old Central Committee) . . . in other words, our guidelines had been worked out, ones that were acceptable to everyone. You say it was a compromise . . .

Yes.

That is always . . . how should I put it? . . . healthy. But they did not keep to this compromise. Why? And here we come to your question: how was it, why was it? What I thought was that we had accepted the November resolution, but in order for us to be able to implement it, an appropriately favourable international atmosphere was needed on the part of the Hungarians, the Poles, the Soviet Union, on the part of Ulbricht – thus, on the part of all five sides. However, obviously, owing to the tragedy that had happened, they did

---

* The resolution of the Party's Central Committee plenum held between 14 and 17 November marked the beginning of the reversal of political and economic reforms instituted in 1968. The resolution blamed right-wing forces for failures in policy which in turn led to Soviet military intervention. It criticized the press for its anti-socialist excesses and declared that the Party's leading role in society was to be strengthened. Dubcek in his address said that the Party would develop further the basic positive aspects of the reform policy, but also that a fight had to be waged against anti-socialist and other extremist forces.

not want to be in contact with me. So I turned it over in my mind; I did not sleep much at night. But luckily I don't need much sleep. When I worked as a district, county or Central Committee Secretary I never slept more than 5 or 6 hours, but that was really the top limit. I never dozed during the day, I have no need to. So, during the nights I kept pondering whether I ought not to resign. For this situation would certainly continue! They were even capable of organizing some kind of provocation if I remained in my post. Another thought occurred to me, but I won't say what that was now. I had a private conversation with someone, you know, which started, or which contributed to, my considering resigning – and making way for someone else.

Who did you speak with?
With a Soviet person. I won't say who it was. So, what I thought was: this situation is going to continue. These thoughts kept coming: the pressures come one after the other and they keep getting stronger. Either there is going to be some kind of show of discontent, and the provocateurs will exploit this, they will organize a blood-bath, and then they will march in once again.... So, I don't know, but in any case what I saw was that 'they' were not willing to normalize co-operation. One day therefore I summoned my assistants from the Secretariat, and I said: I have decided to announce to the Central Committee, to the Presidium, that I would like to leave my post. And I asked them to discuss what I ought to do. Because if we wanted to fulfil the tasks we had taken on (here I was thinking of the November resolution, of all the things that had been accepted and recognized; I was not thinking of the present-day version; at that time another version was in force) . . . in other words, what it was about was that the minimum should be salvageable. Apart from my two assistants, with whom I am still friends today, I also told

Svoboda. Svoboda racked his brains. I am not telling you everything that happened, but this does not mean that I am not telling the truth.

Naturally, you have the right to keep silent about things if you believe that to be right.

I only say this so that you don't think that I am now recounting everything, down to the last word. Well, after some pondering, Svoboda agreed. Apart from this he said something about another matter, which I don't want to mention now, not for the time being. So, what he said was: 'This step would help something that I have in mind. But naturally you won't resign your membership of the Presidium?' I said: 'No, I would like to be present during the implementation of the resolution which we adopted, I would like to take part in implementing what the Central Committee adopted after we came back from Moscow.' Then Cernik got to know about it, and the others, too. I won't go into the details now. We met in session several times. I proposed someone else, not Husak, but to this they again said that perhaps I was wrong, because Husak would be the most acceptable person for the post, for the Soviets as well ... Of course, I now know more than I did at the time. I did not know then that Husak and Bilak had met Brezhnev somewhere in the Ukraine.

When?

From Bilak's reminiscences I know that it was during the time when I was still First Secretary. After the invasion. Bilak divulged this in his memoirs. That is another reason why they are angry with him, because he disclosed many things which he should not yet be making public in his memoirs.

But in the beginning did you trust Gustav Husak?

Well, yes. When he came back, just then the Congress was under way; it had been suspended until we returned from Moscow. Husak made a speech. I had appointed him to head the delegation taking part in the Slovak Communist Party Congress, that is the delegation of Prague CPCZ-Central Committee representatives, but including Barbirek* and others, too. Husak made a speech and sprang to our defence, saying that we had had to sign the Moscow document. But he also said: We don't know who decided on the military intervention, we don't know it to this day. We could not find out even in Moscow.' And he also said: 'Look, what we did is one possible line of direction, a Dubcek line, and one has to say honestly that either we proceed together with Dubcek along the path of implementing this line, or we fall together.' That is how the Congress ended. So this was in August 1968. But in April 1969 I left my post. Well, there were some who mentioned him as well, as a possible successor; I had a different proposal, but I accepted the opinion of the majority of the Presidium, that Husak should be First Secretary. I accepted it – and I became President of the National Assembly. But this is already another chapter! Because they were quite soon to squeeze me out of the post of parliamentary president, as well as from the party Presidium.

And this is the sensitive point. From here on dates, so to speak, the loss of political prestige, the moral loss, and finally the essential loss as well, if I think about the minimum which might have remained from the original conception. Because then the leadership of the CPSU persuaded a few other members of the Presidium, in my opinion, to remove me from the parliamentary function and also from the Presidium.

---

* Frantisek Barbirek was a prominent Slovak Communist politician who opposed Dubcek's reforms, but who faded from public life in the 1970s.

Are we speaking about your colleagues within the party? Who?
I am not naming names, because I don't want to go into it in so much detail. . . .

And how did your expulsion from the Party happen?
I was already surprised by the stances of others of my associates, because they agreed far too easily that I should be squeezed out of the Presidium. They knew me very well. They knew that they would have to confront me with some demand that was too much for me, which exceeded all limits. Because for me the Moscow Protocol was the ultimate limit, and our November decision was the minimum. Lower or higher than that I could not go! And these former colleagues of mine, unfortunately even those who had originally stood up for the revival and the November resolution, who were even willing to agree that the process of renewal had to be continued, took a step which surprised me. They proposed to the Presidium: Let us make a gesture towards the Soviet leadership and let us declare null and void our Central Committee standpoint with regard to the Warsaw letter, as well as our resolution connected with the armed intervention. That was something I could not do. We did not do it even in Moscow, it is not even in the Moscow Protocol, that is why I couldn't do it. They knew this very well, that is why they had put it; because it was clear that I could not accept it. But let's leave out the details. This is where the matter reached a peak, this was the most important phase of the tactics which the Soviet leadership of that time habitually employed. In fact it had not one, but several dozens and several hundreds, of conveyor belts whose purpose was to disintegrate the Czechoslovak Communist Party, if that was their intention.

97

And they did disintegrate it! They did not manage to do so before 1968, but after that they did; up till then they kept trying to disintegrate it. And gradually, in a cunning or a very simple way, they won over various people. It is a pity that they succeeded. Again, I don't want to name names. In any case, the essence of the tragedy is that they managed to break up the Party leadership, and they deepened the crisis by the fact that in the final analysis we diverged later on from the Moscow Protocol. Because in 1970, after I had left, or already after 1969, they assented to things which I would never have swallowed. They agreed to abolish the Action Programme; they adopted the description of the Party leadership as opportunist and revisionist; they adopted all those statements that there had been a counter-revolution, and that 'there would have been a civil war if the troops had not marched in'; that now 'they had managed to save the homeland', and so on and so forth. All this demagoguery, all this stupidity which they dared to say to the face of this cultured and adult nation is much worse than if somebody spits in your face!

But 20 years have elapsed, and Soviet perestroika, glasnost, and all the reforms attached to one name, that of Gorbachev, give you full recompense. History has proved you right, not after your death but while you are still living. This is a rare exception! What do you think about it?

Look, when it is a matter of the Action Programme, of the policy of renewal, of the Party's Central Committee, I relate all these things not to *myself*, but to the whole collective. Because although I was the one who initiated this line at the October plenum of 1967, and who pursued it to the point that this large team, with the collaboration of academics, drew up such a significant document – I nevertheless profess that *it was a collective achievement*. And this collective achievement is so lasting that it remains valid even after twenty years. Though a lot of people say: Why should we go back? In our country many people say: Why should we go back? We ought to go forward! But then I did not want to give this whole interview until I had exhausted all the other possibilities: I wrote to the Party leadership, to the Central Committee, to *Bratislava Pravda*, to *Rude Pravo* – but all these letters remained in the editorial files. So then I told it to *Unita* and on the Voice of America, and elsewhere, too – and then of course they said: You see, you serve bourgeois propaganda, and if you serve bourgeois propaganda, then our enemies praise you, and it follows logically from this that you are a traitor.

We know these voices. . . . But it really isn't worth paying any attention to these descriptions.
But the main thing, of course, is what you also have said . . . .

That history delivers justice.
Justice, yes. That this is a collective achievement, and that is precisely why there is strength in it! Because when it was a question of the Party leading and the government governing, and that we needed a political programme . . . Once we had a political programme, we said this is the main point. And this programme has to be worked out on a scientific basis. In other words, it is not possible for just any First Secretary, or just any leader, to stand up and say: Now it will be like this, and like that, and spell out very precisely just how it will be. Because in reality it won't be like that! It will be the way that is indicated by the best academic results – in the economy, in sociology, in every kind of sphere. Those who work in the Party, in society, their skills and their knowledge, the skills and knowledge of Party members and non-Party members, the skills and knowledge of trade union and youth functionaries, but chiefly the best people in our

academic life, should all take part in this. Well, that is how we did it! That is why the Action Programme has not lost its validity through all this time. Well, isn't it typical that in our country *they do not want to print* the Action Programme *to this very day*, because it is supposed to be opportunist-revisionist! So, they should hand it over to the university students! If it is now becoming possible to study Plekhanov and I don't know who else, then why can't they study the Action Programme? They can't. Because this programme is still called opportunist and revisionist, and the Party leadership of the time is still called 'opportunist and revisionist', and 'wanting to restore capitalism', to drive Czechoslovakia back into capitalism and to tear it away from the Soviet Union. Well, the reason this programme is still valid today is not – as this propaganda claims – because it wanted to tear us away, and so on, but because it *chimed in with the nation's needs*. Because it found a response in the people's minds, because the Party and the people accepted it! I have said that the Czechs, the Slovaks, the Hungarians, the Ukrainians, they all accepted it so spontaneously that it was a marvel. And that is why it has not become obsolete to this day. If they tell us: we won't go back to that, then I say: it isn't true! We can only go forward if we rid ourselves of all the burden which fell on our backs with the military intervention and since.

You frequently mention the Czechs, the Slovaks, the Hungarians, the Ukrainians, the nations, the nationalities, living in Czechoslovakia. What is your opinion about the situation and the rights of the Hungarian nationals in Slovakia?

What I say is this: when I was a county Party Secretary, first in Banska Bystrica and then in Bratislava, it was always in a region where inhabitants of Hungarian nationality also lived. For over four years I was Slovakian First Secretary, and again I kept meeting the same problems. And I believe that if anything in Marx's ideas, and in the thoughts formulated by Engels, is valid, then it is really true that '*a nation which oppresses other nations can not be free*'.

For many years already these things had been clear to me and to the Party's leadership at that time: that the nationality rights of the Hungarians and Ukrainians living in our country were inviolable! These rights must be defended by the constitution. I would say that the Party must also protect the minority nationalities, so that they can live their own national life, be it a question of mother tongue, of culture, of dance, of entertainment, or of mentality, the particular psychological features. For no two people are alike – and the individual nations also have their particular features, if they can keep their inherited forms of behaviour, which are simply a part of them, which they have inherited from their fathers, their grandfathers and which they simply cannot renounce, not even in the era of socialism! Because after all, it is this that makes the Ukrainians Ukrainian, the Slovaks Slovak, the Hungarians Hungarian! That is why it's very important that they should be able to assert all this.

In my view this is a very important and sensitive issue, in connection with which a socialist Marxist party must adopt an entirely unequivocal standpoint. In this matter *not even the slightest injustice must be allowed to occur*! Because if any kind of injustice does occur, that creates a very grave legacy. It is very difficult to commit it and *very difficult to put it right*. Just as it is very difficult to put right the anti-Sovietism that has evolved. Up to 1968 if anyone anywhere let his tongue wag, it was because there were joint military manoeuvres. We said: Let there be joint military maneouvres, why should that bother us? But from time to time people did worry. But when does a real anti-Soviet mood evolve? When the nation is suppressed. And did they suppress it? They suppressed it, they oppressed it. Well, and what comes after action? Reaction! It depends whether it is big or small. If the nation is treated unjustly, then it is obliged instinctively to defend itself. And it does defend itself. In my view the way to proceed in the future is to recognize minority rights unconditionally. I will give you an example. There used to be an opinion that the Eastern Orthodox Church was more 'progressive' than the Greek-Catholic. For this reason, in the period before us, in the Novotny period, they completely eliminated this Church.

In Romania, too.

But when we got into the top posts, we restored the whole thing. Why should we turn the Greek-Catholic Church into the Eastern Church? They both believe in God. God is the same in both religions. It is true that the ceremonies are different, the liturgy is different, but they have one God. So why did we have to harm the Greek-Catholics? You see, this was one of our first steps, that we realized this. And naturally, the situation is similar with the nationalities. Let them have their schools, if that's what they want! Of course, the matter is not that simple. For example, if we were to tear them away completely from the official State languages, then a Hungarian could only go to university in a place where he would always be among Hungarians. But one can not go, for example, to the College of Zvolen if one does not know the official language, including the technical terms, or to any other area not inhabited by Hungarians. So, there are limits such as these, as well. Here everybody must decide for himself. But one thing is certain: this is an exceedingly sensitive issue, and rights must definitely be respected.

I very much wish that the Romanian leaders could hear these words of yours. There these days they brutally oppress the nationality minorities. Do you receive information about these things?

Well, I only know about it from hearsay. I don't know the concrete details. First of all, I do not have any sources; and nowadays I meet only ordinary people, ordinary citizens. But I have heard that there are serious problems. I naturally know what the system there is like, for example compared to the one we introduced when I was still a politician. We had Hungarian schools, we had the Csemadok [cultural-social association of Hungarians in Czechoslovakia], and we supported this movement. And as First Secretary I went among the Csemadok people – in the end I even danced the *csardas* [Hungarian dance], we got on well together, I joined in everything. So that they might feel that I too was a person who recognized them. So I look at it with these eyes. For me it is incomprehensible when I hear that certain nationality rights *should be somehow repressed*. If this were the rule, and if this sort of thing were to occur, then it would be very harmful for the movement. I can not even imagine this, but then I don't know these things in detail. For this reason I keep to the general principle: everything must be done in order that everyone should respect nationality rights.

What does that mean?

First and foremost, that the minority citizen should learn, should have the *possibility* to learn, his mother tongue. That he should be able to dance his dances, sing his songs, safeguard his own culture, go to his own theatre. That he should not lose that part of himself which is Hungarian, those inherited traits – for this *can in no way be dangerous* with regard to socialism! What can be a danger to socialism is precisely if these rights are not respected. That is what Stalin did in the Soviet Union, disregarding the republics and other territories; he suppressed the local initiatives – and just look what is happening there *now*! Partly also things which the Soviet power is naturally obliged somehow to disarm. But this is not because the Soviet leadership is implementing *perestroika*, but because the old crimes *are hitting back*. Therefore, if someone does not respect these rights today, then that will hit back tomorrow or the day after tomorrow. And it hits back in a very unpleasant way. So that is why it is better if the Party takes the lead and itself resolves these problems. Because then people will say: *Yes, that is what we call a proper party*! Which is what the Hungarians in our country used to say in my time. If you had said to the Hungarians living here at that time: Let's get rid of this leadership that proclaims renewal, it's dreadful what they are doing – then these Hungarians would have told you more or less what I am telling you now.

I did ask them.

And they said, did they not, that the renewal was good, correct, necessary. Unfortunately the outcome today, also on the Hungarian side, is different.

I don't know if we'll come back to it, but if not, then I will say it now: I believe that the Hungarian State and Party leadership also has some things that it must re-examine regarding 1968. Because it was different from what happened in 1956 as well. Whether it was on a small or large scale, but there are signatures on the decision. I do not know if at that time the entry was the decision of the Politburo, but I do know that the Premier – he and I had many conversations, we were even once on holiday together – was Jenoe Fock. He is a very serious man, who in my view considered things very carefully. And at the time it surprised me that he resigned. To this day my explanation for this is that at the time the decision on the military intervention was taken, perhaps it may not be certain that it was a corporate decision. I do not know whose decision it was, that of the Politburo or merely of one or two people. And since it was not a Czechoslovak, but a Hungarian, decision – or rather, the decision of the other countries – this problem should be resolved by everybody at home in their own country: the Bulgarians, the Hungarians and the others. And in my view they ought to evolve some kind of standpoint in this connection, as to *just what help they were in 1968*.

The objective 'result' is that *what they did was bad*. The way they should put this right now is that, with regard to our good-neighbourly relations, they should evaluate this matter, too, analyse it, think about it. In my view, since this was their decision and not ours, our Party can not carry out these analyses, for instance the shaping of the standpoint connected with the Hungarian decision of that time. Therefore, the Hungarian Party leadership should also disassociate itself from this improper intervention, which was targeted at an independent state, a fraternal, allied country. All the more so because we had all signed a common document. On my way back from my visit to Hungary I was so taken with Budapest! When I stood there on that podium – after the discussions with the Politburo, after the signing of the agreement about the alliance, about co-operation, about friendship, about mutual assistance – and when I saw the Budapest Party activists, I looked into their eyes and it looked as if they wanted to say to me – how do you say it in Hungarian . . . '*Stay here!*' And then there came all that! So I say frankly, it was rather that I was expecting this side to say *no* to the intervention. No matter the consequences! Even if it meant losing a leading position! I risked my own skin. And not only I, but many others too. But perhaps you should cut this out, if you think it is too sensitive or tactless!

The Hungarian leadership owes a clear answer to this statement of yours.
All right. So: *whom did this help?* And another thing has to be considered: *Did it help the European socialist movement?*

Naturally not.
Which Communist Party did it help? In Spain there were as many as four Communist Parties; now I read, a month ago, that by now there are only three. Two of them have united. But there are still three! And elsewhere, as well. Where is the influence, the unity? So, what happened? Not only was it in Czechoslovakia that the process of renewal stopped for twenty years, but it stopped also in the Soviet Union, in Hungary, too, everywhere. This was the 'result'. In other words, how could a decision have been correct which conserved the system of 'existing socialism', which at that time they forced onto the other Communist Parties as well through Brezhnevite methods? I therefore believe that the Hungarian leadership ought not to have agreed to it! And I don't know whether Comrade Fock* himself feels anything about this? I don't mean whether he considers himself to be guilty. Who knows whether he was even present at such a discussion, or how it ended. I even think – I may be wrong, but I doubt it – that it was the decision of the Hungarian Politburo. In this interview, we mentioned the Warsaw letter, and the standpoint of our Central Committee. You see, we published everything. Couldn't Kadar have published our letter as well? Or did they make it known at the Hungarian Socialist Workers' Party plenum? No. You know, it is not for position that we have to work. We have to work because we serve: we serve the people, we do everything for them.

* Jeno Fock: a leading Hungarian Communist politician, a member of the Party leadership after the suppression of the Hungarian uprising in 1956. He was Hungarian Prime Minister from 1967 to 1975.

We must work in the spirit of socialism, of real internationalist relations, in the token of joining forces, of understanding
between peoples. Because people have to be distinguished not
on the basis of . . . how do you say it in Hungarian? not on
the basis of *how they say it* . . . *No!*, but what they say! The
important thing is not how, but rather *what* they say. And
it does not matter whether a person says this in Hungarian,
Slovak or Czech; that is not the decisive thing, but the content.
And since at that time the Hungarian side said what it did, and
it was not correct, for that reason I am of the opinion that the
truth ought to be spoken in Hungarian as well, and the matter
should be put right.

*I also think the Hungarian leadership will be obliged to debate
these issues, because it is to the Hungarian Party's great shame
that it took part in 1968 in this armed aggression directed
against Czechoslovakia. And today people admit, moreover,
in private conversations they admitted it even then, that this
is to the eternal shame of the Hungarian leadership of that
time. But let us go on. What do you know about, and what
is your opinion of, the current Hungarian reforms? About the
processes leading towards pluralism, about the development of
our system of institutions, about the changes taking place in our
country?*

In my opinion, these things are brought about by life, these
changes are the results of changing life. In my view there is
a certain naturalness in this. Unfortunately we can not return
to the period of twenty years ago. Because, in theory, why did
the events of that time occur in Czechoslovakia? I don't think I
will offend anyone if I say that it was precisely Czechoslovakia
which at that time was the ripest for such a domestic, political,
economic and social reform. Czechoslovakia was the ripest,
because of its situation, its past, and many things besides.

This is a fact.

These things happened not by accident, but by the nature of things. That is why, if you now ask me about the Hungarian reform movement, one can only regret that Hungary also lost twenty years. In my opinion Hungary at that time could also have chosen a different path, on the basis of real fraternity and solidarity, utilizing real reciprocity, and it might have advanced along that path more easily then than it will do now. I for example, am convinced of the following. Of course, at that time there was no appropriate Soviet leadership, but sometimes it is customary to talk in the abstract, so now I will also disregard the actual situation of that time.

So: If at that time a Gorbachevite leadership had headed the Soviet leadership, and if such a movement had come into being in Czechoslovakia, then I am convinced that – if the Soviet leaders had been close to us ideologically, had understood the inevitability of the scientific-technical revolution, the necessity of pluralism, and moreover, if they had understood that there was a need to change the entire system of economic and social direction, the inner life of society – well, I am convinced that in that case *things would not have developed in the way they did.* For where would the Soviet Union be now?! Would it have to face its current difficulties if it had set about the task twenty years ago? No! But, unfortunately, the Gorbachevite leadership is compelled to lug a very weighty legacy. It has been bequeathed a lot of bad things which are not the fault of *perestroika.* Gorbachev now wants to put things in order. And if this setting in order is late in starting then extreme phenomena also emerge, and in many areas, at that; and then it is very, very difficult to keep these in check. Why? Because very many bad things have accumulated – in nationality policy, in the economy, in culture, in human relations – and it is difficult to deal with them.

I welcome what is happening in Hungary today. Because it really is a question of a seeking for the path which leads to the real renewal of socialism. It is a question of a socialist platform. Of course, we have to be clear that *in society it is never possible for everything to be strictly socialist*. Other people want to live as well, they want to be able to express themselves, right from the Churches to I don't know who. Since it is absurd if, on the one hand, the constitution declares freedom of religion, and on the other hand an ordinary citizen is afraid to have his child christened; he'd rather go to church in the neighbouring village, or I don't know where. If he has the right, then *let him really have the right*. In my view the Church can fulfil a very useful mission – in educating people, in improving relations between people. If a person has the right to be an atheist, then he also has the right to be religious. Therefore, what I can see is that the processes taking place in Hungary profoundly affect the social system, and something new is being born. These things may yet go through a transformation. Because, you know, things don't always happen exactly the way one plans them. Life can bring about something else. And, as I have already said, if something is late in starting, with a time lag, then the situation is tense to the point of explosion. One can not be surprised if something somewhere cracks, breaks, if things do not go in such a way that people respect the 'big socialist framework', which allegedly marks out precisely that you can only go from here to there.

The main thing is that, in the pluralistic manifestations, one has to find the healthy optimum of a socialist programme, so that in this programme everyone can find his place. That people should praise the Party! Because some people say: The Communist Party must be eliminated, and that will lead to the renewal. Well, there won't be any renewal. There won't be anything. Some people will pursue this line even if the Party goes before them and has reform intentions, and they want to dismiss the leadership, which is incapable of resolving everything from one day to the next. Since in this system of ours the Communist Party is called to put the renewal into realization. It is another question that it is not doing this – because there are places where to this day it is not doing it. But the Communist Party has to do this! It has to renew itself! It has to aim at this renewal even if it loses some of its former positions. But it has to do it; what is more, *it must even put the knife into its own flesh, even if it hurts*. It must cut out what is unhealthy, cut it out of the healthy body. People say that by this the Party loses something. But in actual fact, and in the last resort, it will not lose anything, because people will say: Yes, this is now a real party. We will follow this party. We shall vote for this party, because this party has introduced such or such beneficial reforms, good mechanisms; this is what we need!

So, I wish the Hungarians success. Of course, things don't always turn out as one imagines, but I believe that if we surmount the difficulties, of which there is an abundance in the Soviet Union, in our country and everywhere, there will in the end be success in renewing socialism, so that it creates something new. Because too many blows, far too many blows, have been levelled at socialism!

Thank you.
[Well, with this we finish the lengthy interview, all the eight cassettes, all the three hours.

We were more tired than Dubcek. He was visibly elated because he was able to speak his mind without haste, in depth and in detail.]